WHOM SHALL I MARRY?

A QUESTION OF VITAL CONCERN TO YOUNG CHRISTIANS, THEIR PARENTS AND THE CHURCH

by
Dorothy Voshell

PRESBYTERIAN AND REFORMED PUBLISHING CO.
PHILLIPSBURG, NEW JERSEY

This book is dedicated to my faithful, loving husband, Frank

Presbyterian & Reformed Publishing Co.
Box 817, Phillipsburg, N.J. 08865

ISBN: 0-87552-509-1

PRINTED IN THE UNITED STATES OF AMERICA

CONTENTS

PREFACE

''Whom shall I marry?'' or, as we usually, ungrammatically, say today, ''Who shall I marry?,'' is a question every Christian contemplating marriage *must* answer before God. The question must be answered apart from rationalization, emotional feeling or any other unbiblical motivation. Surely every Christian should want his or her question, "Whom shall I marry?," answered only by God. If this book settles that question for only one person, I will be happy. If many should be influenced to choose only Christian mates, I would be happier still. But my pleasure is not the most important thing—God's is. And when He is pleased, our pleasure is certain.

In this day when even some evangelicals are questioning the inerrancy and infallibility of Scripture on some points, I take my stand without apology upon the presupposition that God has revealed Himself and His will for us in Scripture. My position rests upon Scripture chiefly as interpreted by men of a Reformed persuasion, that is, according to the doctrines of the Protestant Reformation. For exegesis of Scripture I have relied upon them because they know Greek and Hebrew and I do not.

I trust that every conviction of mine expressed here is biblical, resting not upon personal suppositions but upon God's Word, for there alone are His absolutes for all of life, marriage being one of the most important decisions in our Christian life. Only His Word is the final authority giving purpose, meaning and reality to marriage. Just as we never choose anything else in life without considering certain standards—a new car, grapefruit, plumbing, medical treatment—we need to follow certain standards in choosing a mate. God has given us the rules to follow.

May God use this book to help you choose the lifetime mate He has chosen for you. Also, I pray that parents will more clearly see their responsibility to God; to the Church, the bride of Christ; to her members and to those in authority in their local churches for the marriage of their sons and daughters. And may each of us have renewed interest, interaction, communication and involvement with—and love for—any member of His body who is facing the decision to marry.

I owe much to many Christian friends who have fervently prayed for this book: my faithful typist, Emily Roach; my constantly supportive husband and best critic, Frank; my children and my two cherished pastors, Robert Auffarth and William Mahlow, Jr., who have faithfully encouraged me—even urged me—to write this book. They, too, see the deep need for us genuinely to discover God's answers as to who should be our 'Adam' or 'Eve.'

Unless otherwise indicated, Scripture quotations are taken from the New American Standard Bible, published by the Lockman Foundation.

INTRODUCTION

Books on marriage are not something new. There are hundreds on the market filled with Christian and non-Christian advice for happy marriages. So you may honestly think that another book on the subject is only adding to the writing of books of which there seems to be no end, as Solomon once said. But I believe it is time to profoundly rethink some particular aspects in the spiritual spectrum of marriage. That is the chief concern of this book; therefore you will find little said about the physical or material sides of marriage, not because they are unimportant, but because there are many fine Christian books adequately dealing with those subjects.

I am hoping that this book will fill a particular need for Christian young people who are dating with (or without) the intention to marry—an urgent need which I think merits the serious consideration of these young people and their parents who say their children belong to Jesus Christ. It is of vital necessity to know in depth *why* a Christian must marry "only in the Lord." Beyond a simple demand, "Don't marry an unbeliever," we must be willing and able to explain *why*. And, though important, it is not enough just to tell our children the effects of mixed marriage upon them and their children: they must also consider the effects upon our God and His bride, the Church of Christ, and the inevitable effect upon society. They must see the tragedy of such union as God sees it.

Today the Church witnesses an appalling number of her young people being unequally yoked with unbelievers—in spite of the fact God has told believers to marry "only in the Lord." I say 'appalling' because such marriages do frighten me. I am afraid for the couples involved, for their covenant children, for society in general; but most of all, I am appalled at what such mixed marriages do to the Church of Christ—both the universal body, and its local congregations. I am dismayed at the example set for other young Christians; at the failure of church officers to warn and discipline before it is too late; at the number of parents who never discuss their children's dating habits with their pastors or elders—who actually cooperate in uniting their believing child with an unbeliever; and, sad to say, some pastors who, by not exercising discipline, aid and abet such marriages which are totally contrary to God's command. Our disobedience has dreadful consequences which I hope to illustrate from Scripture and from life today—biblical, empirical evidence of the great harm done to homes, children and the Church.

Much has been written on marriage and sex dealing with the cultural, psychological and physical aspects of the marriage relationship. Some Christian books and manuals warn of the suffering and heartache incurred by the Christian and unbeliever who marry. But what about our wonderful, sovereign God and His Church? How are they affected? What damage is done?

Answers to these questions are to be found only in His Word. Only there will we find what the Church means to God and thus what we mean to Him. Only there may we look for directives and discipline for every area of life. His wisdom and understanding are to be applied to every facet of our lives. But in this book we are primarily concerned to discover how God's wisdom, understanding and discipline apply to whom we date and whom we marry. Must we take God seriously? Or can we consider that marriage is a private matter and so personal an area that we can safely lean to our own understanding or romantic feelings? Is that very first date with one of His dear children of no concern to Him who has counted the very hairs of our heads and who Himself lives within each of us who love Him?

The conviction that something more needs to be said about the marriage of unbeliever to believer is motivated by my concern for the body of Christ, the honor of God and for my own children and the children of the Church. I feel that I can help. I have had the privilege of learning from great men of Reformed persuasion who had, or have, a profound awareness of the meaning of marriage, the Church and our relationship to Christ as believers. Raising a family of seven children has been a real eye-opener; counseling them and their many friends as well as teaching youth groups and serving as an elder's wife for about 25 years have contributed much to my experience and knowledge. I would like to share these insights with you in the hope that you will be helped as parents and young people to see a little more clearly why marriage is so important to God. Most of all, I hope that you finish this book with the conviction that you must marry only a man or woman who is bought by the precious blood of Christ.

I said that primarily I address Christians. That is not to say that I do not hope those who do not know Christ in a personal way will read this book. On the contrary, if you do not know Christ as your Lord and Saviour and you happen to read these lines, I hope that you will come to see what true Christian marriage is, that you will be motivated by the Holy Spirit to love Christ, and that you will recognize that only the home established on Jesus Christ pleases God. That is the only reason for everything we are and do—His pleasure and glory. Marriage must glorify Him, our triune God.

It may be that whether you are a believer or not the very thought of being limited to God's narrow choice of mates among believers in Christ may be alien—even repugnant—to you. You may feel that union to another human being in Christian marriage—or any other marriage for that matter—is restricting and suffocating, leaving you with no 'freedom' to form new relationships outside the bonds of matrimony. But a little introspection and total honesty with yourself, particularly if you've suffered the dissolution of a temporary man-woman relationship, might reveal a deep-down desire for a permanent union, which is the only kind God ever endorsed. This desire is admitted by many who have been disillusioned in their belief that marriage is not necessary for two people who "love" each other. I think of a very lovely "liberated" young woman who had had numerous love affairs. In an interview on television she wistfully confessed that she hoped one day to marry a fine man, have a home and bear children. She yearned for stability and security.

Woman ". . . longs for that indescribable, ultimate fulfillment . . .all long for, pursue and sometimes experience the indefinable something that is more than the flesh. It is the whole fruit of love—as in a peach, not just the sweet flesh, but its aroma, skin, pit, shape, color—the very peachness of the peach; the whole peach."[1]

Certainly men have the same yearnings for wholeness: the peachness of the peach. And certainly the wholeness of Christian marriage cannot be experienced when Christ is absent from the heart of one partner. Then, instead of being a whole peach, marriage is often much like the fruit that Arabs call ushar. Native to parts of the Dead Sea Valley, ushar resembles an orange or apple—pleasant to see and to touch. If struck or pressed, it explodes like a puffball, leaving only fragments of rind and fibers in your hand. The apparent wholeness and beauty is only an illusion.

Jesus Christ is the only one who gives God's "aroma, skin, pit, shape, color" to marriage. Indeed, He is its very essence and solidarity. He alone makes people whole. Two whole persons make a complete marriage. My prayer for you is that you experience this wholeness; that you and your parents will better understand how much you mean to Christ and the Church; that you may more clearly see why you must never consider marrying anyone who does not belong to Christ.

---

[1] Harriet La Barre, "When Women Find Sex Disappointing," *Ladies Home Journal*, November 1976, p. 192.

1

YOUR PLACE IN THE CHURCH

Before we can ever grasp the significance, the beauty or the meaning of Christian marriage, we must have a good understanding of the meaning of the bride of Christ, for it is to this relationship of Christ to His Church that our Christian marriages are likened by God's Word. If ever you are to understand why God commands believers to marry "only in the Lord" (I Cor. 7:39), you must realize with mind and heart who you are in the body of Christ for it is this relationship to Christ which determines whom you are to marry. This command is not just an arbitrary order to limit your freedom of choice; God leaves you free to choose the one He intends for you—the right one who loves Him, too.

An understanding of the identity and structure of the Church and your place in it necessarily involves some theology[1] and ecclesiology (doctrine[2] about the Church). Though you may at this moment think that we could well dispense with this chapter because it bodes to be boring . . . please . . . stay with me and read on to get the whole exciting picture. This chapter *is* essential to lay the proper foundation for an answer to the book's question.

You may truly love Christ as Saviour, trust Him as your substitute for sin, desire to honor Him and grow to be like Him, yet perhaps you have never fully understood where you fit into the Church or even what the Church really is. I want to help you to think carefully about the Church as she existed in the Old and New Testaments. I'm going to ask you to do something you may never have done (or thought of doing) before. As we talk of Christ's bride, His body, and meet some of her members in the Scriptures, I would like you to think to yourself: "These people are *my* relatives—brothers and sisters in Christ. They are part of His body, too. How I should like to meet these people of God and talk with them. They really are more closely related to me than my own earthly family—brothers, sisters, children, Dad or Mom. Imagine that!"

I have found that looking at myself as a close relative of both Old and

---

[1] It is regrettable and ironic that other "ologies"—psychology, biology, anthropology, etc.—are generally considered to be intriguing, while theology and ecclesiology are many times regarded as dry and dispensable. Though it should be the other way round, the study of man generates more enthusiasm than the study of God which often seems about as appetizing as a plate of fried wood chips. This certainly doesn't prove that we love God more than ourselves, does it?

[2] Doctrine simply means "teaching."

New Testament characters who had saving faith—say, Abraham, Joseph, David, Peter, Paul, Dorcas—I experience a wonderful feeling of kinship, a belonging and security in the continuum of the Church (as recorded from Genesis to Revelation) from before the foundation of the world through time and eternity.

Another thing you can do to increase your appreciation for, and trust in, God's plan for you in His body is to take each promise made to His people for yourself (except, of course, the ones fulfilled for Israel in particular—for example, Israel's occupation of literal Canaan). When God says to Israel, "I will be a God to you and to your children," we parents and children can say, "He means that for *me*." When He says, "I have loved you with an everlasting love" (Jer. 31:3) and "I will be the God of all the families of Israel [the Church today], and they shall be my people," He is talking to you and to me. When He says, "Israel is my possession," you can say, "That means *me*." Or when God tells Israel that He is their beloved Husband, we can exultantly wonder, "Why, that means *me* because I am part of His bride. In His electing love His relationship to me is the same as that to those who loved Him in Old Testament times. I am His and He is mine forever."

The Christ foreshadowed and prophesied in the Old Testament is presented in the New Testament as the Lord of the covenant. Old Testament believers looked forward to, and were saved by faith in, the provision Christ made for their sins (Rom. 4:3); we in New Testament times look back upon the perfect sacrifice He made for us.

God said to the nation Israel, "You only have I known of the families of the earth: therefore I will visit upon you all your iniquities" (Amos 3:2, ASV). He says the same thing to us, the Church, today. He has chosen us chiefly as families—but individually, too—covenanting with us to be our God. With the covenant comes responsibility on the part of His chosen ones to be holy, separate people. If we aren't, we can expect His righteous indignation.

I hope that this gives you a little idea of how you can actively relate to God's people as you read from Genesis to Revelation, considering yourself a beloved one in His plan, just as beloved as each lover of God you meet in His Word. If you relate in this way to the Israel of the Old Testament and to the Church of the New Testament (both of them the same body of Christ—the bride), you can't help but love your God more and more and have a better appreciation of your relationship to Him as His bride![3] God's love,

---

[3]I am not in any way implying that Jewish people are not included in the covenant with Christ. No, indeed. As Paul vigorously protested, Israel is not cast off now. Every Jew who

His promises, warnings and commandments are like Himself. They have no "variation or shifting shadow"; they are constant and true as God is;[4] we can depend on them because He is changeless.

Let's go on to our discussion of the Church, of which you are a vital part. As we do, you keep thinking of *your* place in His body,[5] *your* relationship and *your* responsibility to Him and to other members of His body. You must not think of yourself as a saved but somehow separate entity, off to yourself, "doing your own thing."[6] You belong to *Him* now, and to *me* and to all those (past or present) who love Him; you belong, in other words, to the family of God, the household of faith.

The Bible tells us that the Church consists of all who wear the robes of Christ's righteousness, that they are washed in the blood of the Lamb of God who takes away the sin of the world.[7] If you believe that Jesus Christ died to pay the penalty for your sin, and you love Him as Lord of your life, you have been born again into this family of God, this elect race, a royal priesthood, a holy nation (the new Israel), a people for God's own possession to "show forth the excellencies of Him" who has called us "out of darkness into His marvelous light" (I Pet. 2:9, 10).

Peter tells us that we who love Jesus are living stones in the temple of God, the invisible Church. Jesus Christ is the chief cornerstone in this temple. The living stones rest completely on Him as their foundation; we cannot be displaced. That expression, "living stones," has always filled my heart with awe, because I know that my heart was once hard and dead, cold as stone, but now it is alive because the Holy Spirit gave it life—the new birth. God indwells our souls; a miracle of His power alone makes us living stones. To think of seeing a stone come to life and think and talk and see and feel and worship God—believers are surely miracles of His grace, nothing less!

In I Corinthians 12 Paul sets before us in the most graphic way our place in the body of believers. He tells us that though we are many members we are one in Christ, using our spiritual and material gifts for each other, needing each other's help and love and fellowship, caring for one another,

---

accepts Jesus Christ as Lord and Saviour is a member of the new Israel. In Him there is neither Jew nor Gentile. Paul, Jesus, and the apostles recognized that the Church has its roots in the Old Testament.

[4] James 1:17.

[5] Ephesians 1:22, 23.

[6] Ephesians 2:18-22; Romans 12:4,5.

[7] Isaiah 61:10; Revelation 7:9, 13.

suffering when another member suffers or falls into sin, rejoicing in blessings from God.

In Ephesians 4:25 Paul again reminds us that we are members one of another. Because we are loved equally by God, Paul cautions us in Romans 12 not to think more highly of ourself than of other members in the body, for, he says, "So we being many are one body in Christ, and every one members of another." We have different gifts. So we are to *serve* each other with our gifts and our love and affection and prayers.

Just as God called Old Testament Israel and covenanted to be a God to her and her children, so He covenants with His bride, the new Israel, to be a God to us and to our children. Don't you marvel that Jesus calls His bride His own body? Paul says it is a great mystery, yet this is how close to Him you and I are as believers in Christ.

Now this body of Christ is holy in His sight, set apart for Himself. He tells us that He is in the midst of His people—Jews and Gentiles who love Him. Even at this moment Jesus prays for us to be kept holy while in this world. The holiness given to each member of His body was earned for us by Jesus Himself: He lived a perfectly holy, sinless life for us and died a sacrificial death to pay for and remove our sin. This holiness is our dearest possession and treasure because without it we could never live in God's presence nor behold the face of our dear Saviour. We could never know and love God as Father in a personal way nor enjoy the blessed presence of the Holy Spirit in our beings. This holiness of Christ sets us apart from the world—not out of it but apart from it. God dwells with us and in us. We are the apple of His eye.

Separation from sin makes demands upon all of our activities and interests. Nothing may subtly or overtly divert affection, allegiance or obedience from our triune God. Nothing may be given priority above Him. Nothing. Not money, fame, prestige, talents, father, mother, children—nor wives, nor husbands.

We must never forget that we have not first chosen God. No! God the Father first chose us to be a special people for His Son. This relationship transcends all others yet makes every other personal relationship a beautiful reflection of God's loving, sacrificial relationship to us.

Christian marriage is patterned on this intimate union of us to Christ. Husbands are to love their wives as Christ loves His bride (Eph. 5:25). He loved His bride so strongly and eternally that He gave His life a ransom for her sin so that she would be pure and radiant for holy union with Him. His affection and love belong to her forever. In gratitude the Church willingly submits to His loving, sacrificial headship—not slavishly as a serf, but willingly and joyfully as part of His body.

This teaches us how holy human marriage is and why it should be permanent until death separates us. As wives we are to be subject to a loving husband as the Church is to Christ her Bridegroom. This subjection is not tyranny; it is submission to a yoke of sacrificial love under the authority that God has given a husband, the head of the home. Jesus said that His yoke is easy and His burden is light, and that is exactly how easily and gently the authority of a loving husband should rest upon his wife—she is neither oppressed nor inferior. The Church loves Christ because He first loved her; a bride loves her husband because he loves her in the Lord.

Paul says this is a great mystery how the Church is one body with Christ.[8] Just so, how great a mystery, that two human beings who are married become one in the Lord. Therefore husbands are to love their wives just as they love their own bodies, God tells us. They must be willing to die for their wives as Christ was willing to die for the Church.

Human marriage is to reflect and express this oneness of Christ and His Church. It is to mirror the intense, sacrificial love of the Lord for His bride. No wonder God insists—more than that, commands—that believers marry only in the Lord. This is the only way true oneness of love and spirit can be achieved.

God will never approve any bond of fellowship with another which in any way profanes our relationship to our Bridegroom. Indeed, God denounces us as covenant breakers when we rebel against His commands. That's what He called His covenant people, Israel—covenant breakers. There were a lot of covenant breakers in Old Testament times, and there are still a lot of us who are covenant breakers today, putting idols—not the

---

[8]This body of Christ must not be confused with Christ's physical body which died for our sins and arose a glorified body. Dr. Clowney says, "If we understand the grounding of the body figure in Christ's giving of his own body as covenantal representative, we will escape many misconceptions. We will not identify the church with the resurrection body of Christ. Christ has a literal resurrection body."

To be in Christ's body means that we are "represented by Christ in His work of redemption." We are "found in him" (Phil. 3:9, 10). Christ arose from the dead on our behalf and we are united representatively in His body. Clowney says: "They are one in Christ's body; they are one body in Christ (Romans 12:5); they are a body of Christ . . . (I Corinthians 12:27); they are the body of Christ (Ephesians 4:12)." "The figure of the body of Christ stands against the background of covenantal headship." (The above quotations are from Edmund Clowney, *The Doctrine of the Church* [Philadelphia: Presbyterian and Reformed Publishing Co., 1969], pp. 40-41.)

least of which is an unbelieving mate—before our God. Oh, we don't think of Christians in this day and age as covenant breakers, but we are.

In the war between good and evil, between the forces of Satan and Christ's bride, the Christian constantly battles against evil, his new nature against the old sinful nature with all of its sinful desires. Satan with diabolical cunning, exploits our weaknesses.[9] He never tires of making ridiculous imitations of God's beautiful gifts and institutions—especially love and marriage. Indefatigably he labors to divert our God given feelings and sexual desires to ignoble or base purposes. He knows that once he can turn our desire to those who do not love Christ, or to other idols, we will begin to rationalize, defend our bad conscience, sin against our God and forget our covenant obligations to God.

This is exactly what happened to Israel so many times. One example is when Balak, King of Moab, urged Balaam, the false prophet, to curse Israel.[10] Balaam finally demonstrated to Balak that it was impossible for him to bring curses upon God's chosen ones, but he thought of a more effectual way to seduce Israel from their God: the charms of the beautiful women of Moab and Midian. The Scriptures say that the dumb ass Balaam rode showed more wisdom than his master. But Balaam was no dummy as Satan's serf when it came to knowing the easiest, craftiest way to turn Israel to idolatry. No bloodshed. No violence. Israel would not even suspect their peril inasmuch as the way to ruin would be so exciting and pleasurable: good food, beautiful women, and titillation of mind and spirit in forbidden friendship with strange gods.

So the men of Israel were invited to the sacrifices of the gods of Moab and Midian. And they ate. And then, they bowed down to their gods. "Israel joined himself to Baal-Peor." The Bible wastes no words: they were invited, they ate, they bowed, they joined. The progression *away* from God was immediate and fatal. They committed spiritual whoredom, these members of the congregation of God, Christ's body. They were conquered more easily by lust for beautiful women and their false gods than by the armies of Moab. They were almost in the land of Canaan where they could feast on God's favor. Yet they threw it all away because they did not treasure their covenant standing with the only true God.

This shows us how we can so easily despise God's marvelous, gracious

---

[9] Acts 13:10—Paul spoke of Elymus the sorcerer as a child of the devil, perverting the right ways of the Lord, just as Satan does.

[10] See Numbers 22.

covenant. This same despising of God's covenant is evident when a Christian marries an unbeliever; shame and grief is brought upon the whole body of Christ. In the final analysis, such lack of concern for the grace God has shown is in reality lack of fervent love for God. We see this lack of love and dearth of gratitude for His covenant today just as plainly as we see it in all of the biblical accounts of Israel's neglect of God.

We are shocked when we learn from Scripture that Solomon, who at one time cherished wisdom above every other treasure, could foolishly stoop to idolatry. He even built altars to false gods. Whatever influenced this wisest of men to so heinously betray the God of the covenant? The answer: his heathen wives did; they swayed him to such foolishness (Neh. 13:25-27).

Yes, we are shocked at wise Solomon's behavior, forgetting that he belonged to Christ's bride, but we do the same thing. We forget who we are. And perhaps in a moment of forgetfulness—in a moment of coldness and indifference toward God—we date an unbeliever and the next thing we know, we are married to one. Instead of giving allegiance to our God, we transfer our allegiance to this thing we call "love," as C. S. Lewis says. And then our passionate love for another, when we make it our god, becomes a "demon which destroys us." That's what happened to Solomon.

God was justly angry with Israel whose "whoredom" (God doesn't mince words or use euphemisms) turned God against them, something Balaam couldn't do with all his prophecies and enchantments. A plague broke out and many people died.

Doesn't plague of some sort always follow defection from God? Both kinds of adultery had been committed—spiritual and physical. Spiritual adultery or unfaithfulness to God who has called Himself our Husband gives rise to all kinds of evil. In Ezekiel 16 God speaks of Israel's spiritual adultery which finally led the people of God to the place of sacrificing their children to false idols. God sent Ezekiel to Israel to remind them of their miserable, deplorable beginnings. He reminds them of His favor and the honors He had bestowed on them. He points out their treacherous and ungrateful departure from Himself, which He calls adultery and impudent whoredom.

How the Israelites must have hated to hear Him remind them of how He had taken them into covenant with Himself; beautified and adorned them; plentifully fed them; given them a reputation among the nations; made them His wife, saving them from ruin. He loved them even though there was nothing in them or about them to love. After leaving their God, their true love, Israel's idolatry led them into deeper and deeper involvement in wickedness. They had honored the false religions of their neighbors until they actually grew fond of the idols. In mercy God warned them before He brought judgment upon them. They didn't heed. He even tried to bring them to their senses by allowing the hated Philistines to ridicule their ways. Even though the Philistines were idolators themselves, they scorned the lewd conduct of the Israelites. But Israel wouldn't repent, so God had to bring about their ruin. Surely there is a lesson here for us, the bride of Christ, to learn today.

Israel committed spiritual adultery with foreign idols. In almost every instance this was the result of marriage to lovers of foreign gods. These alliances with the enemies of God caused God's children to break their marriage contract with God.

As the true spiritual Israel, do we really think we don't, or won't, commit spiritual adultery when we wilfully seek an alliance in marriage to an unbeliever who worships another god? We may try to assure ourselves over and over that it is not our intention to be unfaithful to God, but how can we convince ourselves that we will not succumb to the influence of an unbelieving mate when most evidence points in that direction? I don't believe that we can squirm out of our covenant responsibility so easily. No. We are a holy possession of His, united to Him for eternity. We must see this clearly so that we cherish the miracle of our relationship to Jesus as His bride.

I believe we are cold and thankless as covenant people because we have stopped learning. Often we don't realize who we are, how much God loves us; we don't really love Him enough for making us His own, for making us kings and queens who will rule with Him forever. From before the foundations of the world He has chosen us to be His "treasure people."[11] He has adorned us with spiritual gems: holiness and special honor above all people. Like Israel of old He has clothed us in righteousness, washed us from our sins, beautified us in Christ, saved us from perdition.

Shall we betray this lover of our souls who has called Himself our Husband? Shall we, dare we, bring disgrace upon the bride of Christ, blemishing and marring her, by uniting ourselves with unbelievers? Of course not. We are bound to Him and to every brother and sister in Christ by the precious blood of His covenant. The whole body of Christ—the past, present and future—belongs to us and we belong to them in Christ. Our relationship to Jesus and to each other supersedes every other human tie on earth. As living stones we support each other in the building. No stone is

[11] Edmund Clowney, *The Doctrine of the Church*, p. 11.

too small to matter. If one is hurt or broken, the whole structure is weakened.

I believe if young people and parents *really* hear God's loving overtures, with heart as well as mind, and if they have a genuine understanding of who they really are in His body, then we will see a true concern that children of the covenant marry only "in the Lord."

God calls to you and to me today, "My covenant child, don't marry out of the Lord. I love you. You are mine. Put me first. Don't call down my judgment upon you."

2
IS YOUR MARRIAGE A PRIVATE MATTER?

Yes, it is our own personal affair, say most young people today—Christian young people, too. Many parents agree—Christian parents, too; and they, with their children, resent any intrusion or suggestions to the contrary by friends, relatives, pastors or their session of church elders.

What is the reason for this? It was not always so. Within just my lifetime there has been a shift from considering marriage as a somewhat public concern, to considering it a solely private matter. Why?

Francis Schaeffer says, "Our Western post-Christian world has been undercut by . . . liberal theology."[1] I, about the same age as Dr. Schaeffer, have seen this undercutting by liberal theology (or "humanism," for clearer labeling) which places human thinking before God's thinking. I have seen God's Word more and more replaced by man's wisdom—man's idea of God, of ethics, of morality.

Like it or not, aware of it or not, liberal thought has affected young and old, Christian and non-Christian. We are all more or less tarred by the stick of liberalism, or humanism. Modern secular thought no longer considers God to be in the picture, much less to be a sovereign God. If mentioned at all, He is merely a God of the imagination or experience of men, not the God and Father of our Lord Jesus Christ, the triune God revealed to us in His Word.

All of us have to some extent imbibed this humanistic philosophy. It pervades everything in our lives: politics (Watergate is an example), the arts, our work ethics, recreation, religion, psychiatry, medicine, psychology, literature, sex and marriage (marriage, of course, being the primary concern of this book).

All of us are to some extent affected by this prevailing philosophy that man is in control; we may decide what is best for us apart from God's wishes—in business, in worship, in marriage, for example. And courtship and marriage are usually considered to be in the most personal, private category of all. "My decisions are personal and private," we hear constantly, "nobody's business except my own . . . . Most especially I may marry whom I wish (or sleep with whom I wish, without marriage) as long as we love and no one else is hurt."

---

[1]Francis Schaeffer, *The Church at the End of the Twentieth Century* (Downers Grove, Ill.: Inter-Varsity Press, 1970), p. 126.

When man's will is substituted for God's will, then our actions are motivated by our own private desires; desire is translated into action which, we convince ourselves, is no one else's business.

Now we Christians, too, are affected by this way of thinking. As a believer, how many times have you assured yourself that a course of action you've decided upon is your private matter with no effect upon anyone else? Isn't it true that today's books, TV shows, philosophers, psychologists and many religious leaders encourage this attitude?

Almost every panel discussion I see and hear on television and radio is dominated by one man-made "absolute": "*I* think"; "this is *my personal* opinion." And each person's opinion seems to be considered valid. No mention is made of the only true absolute, our sovereign God who has revealed Himself and His absolute standards in His inerrant Word. *Man* is his own guide and sets his own standards. Each is a law to himself. This is humanism.

Shouldn't we be weeping for this sad state of affairs, particularly for the fact that Christian young people—and many of their parents—are influenced by this egocentric philosophy when selecting a life partner?

I weep, and have wept many times. I cry when I see fine young believers in Christ choose mates who do not love their Lord. I grieve for their parents, for many of them are grief-stricken, too, and for those who side with their children's unscriptural decisions (even to the point of leaving their churches). I have lamented the lack of church discipline in some of these cases. I have mourned the rebellion of both children and parents toward efforts of pastors and sessions to lovingly enforce discipline.

Do you say, "Well, we deserve happiness; we are so much in love"? Do parents agree, "Yes, they do deserve happiness"?

Innately, most of us feel that, of all things, marriage promises ultimate happiness—sublime sexual happiness in particular, and other blessings in general. Other things—money, fame, good health—promise happiness too, but a little less happiness than marriage affords. Marriage is a different thing, the queen of happiness. We don't want to miss out on its joys. As long as we have a legal right to marry whom we please, we will let nothing stand in our way—not parents, not God. We have our rights! As one man once said, when speaking of a sinful decision he made, "A man has a right to happiness. I had to take my one chance when it came."

Remember, I am writing for Christians first of all. The presupposition here is that you as a Christian consider marriage absolutely indispensable as the framework for sexual activity. You are concerned with the moral obligations of sex, but perhaps you consider your marriage your own private affair. And even though your marriage to an unbeliever is a breach of your faith and disobedience to God, you mean to go through with such a union because you deserve happiness.

C. S. Lewis said, "A right to happiness doesn't, to me, make much more sense than the right to be six feet tall, or to have a millionaire for a father, or to get good weather whenever you want to have it."[2]

We would be shocked if anyone defended a person who makes illegal money because it makes him happy. A child enjoying stolen cookies is very happy for the moment, but in the wrong, no matter how guileless his cherubic face. No, true happiness never comes by ignoring God's rules. True joy and contentment come when we do the right things, in sex and marriage too.

Instead of snatching happiness as our right, we must receive happiness as a gift from God because we have obeyed Him. Pure delight, His Word says, comes from keeping His law. True, lasting happiness comes to us no other way. Besides, *our* happiness is not the "summum bonum," but the glory of the triune God is.

Is your marriage a private matter, a matter which affects only *your* happiness? God doesn't think so. For one example, Ezra, an Old Testament priest, held God's people of Israel responsible for mingling the seed of believers and unbelievers. It was not a private matter. The congregation of Israel was affected in a vital, fundamental way. Each member was joined to the other members of Israel by the ties of God's grace, and what one member did affected that whole body of the congregation.

In chapter 9 Ezra tells us that the princes came to him saying, "The people of Israel and the priests and the Levites have not separated themselves from the people of the lands [the heathen], according to their abominations . . . . they have taken some of their daughters as wives for themselves and for their sons, so that the holy race [Israel then, believers today] has intermingled with the peoples of the lands . . ." (vv. 1-2).

Fathers and sons were guilty. Ezra says, "When I heard about this matter, I tore my garment and my robe . . . and sat down appalled. Then everyone who trembled at the words of the God of Israel on account of the unfaithfulness of the exiles gathered to me, and I sat appalled until the evening offering" (vv. 3-4).

---

[2]C.S. Lewis, "We Have No 'Right to Happiness' " in *God in the Dock* (Grand Rapids: W. B. Eerdmans Publishing Co., 1972), p. 318.

Ezra and those who feared the Lord were horrified because of the unfaithfulness of God's covenant people. He told God that he was ashamed and embarrassed to lift up his face to Him because their sins had risen above their heads, and their guilt had grown even to the heavens. He admitted to God that because of the sin of intermarriage to unbelievers, the kings and priests were given into the hand of the kings of the lands. They had been captured and plundered and put to open shame.

In all of this slavery, Ezra praised God's mercy and love given in spite of their sin, but he confessed that they had broken God's commandment to have nothing to do with the heathen: the Canaanites, Hittites, Perizzites, Jebusites, Ammonites, Moabites, Egyptians and Amorites. This commandment was given, not because the people were of a different race than the Israelites. Racial prejudice was not the issue; it was not a matter of Jew versus another Semitic people. Rahab, the harlot of Jericho, and Ruth the Moabitess both became believers and married Israelites with God's blessing; they were both believing converts.

In his prayer to God, Ezra repeats the command of God which they had broken: "So now do not give your daughters to their sons nor take their daughters to your sons, and never seek their peace or their prosperity, that you may be strong and eat the good things of the land and leave it as an inheritance to your sons forever" (v. 12).

Perhaps you are saying, "Well, that was in Old Testament times. Does that hold true for us in these New Testament days?"

Yes, God says the same thing to you today, except that our inherited land is the reality of heaven (the heavenly Jerusalem) pictured by the land of the Israelites. In different words God commands in II Corinthians 6:14, 15: "Do not be bound together with unbelievers; for what partnership have righteousness and lawlessness, or what fellowship has light with darkness? Or what harmony has Christ with Belial, or what has a believer in common with an unbeliever?" (As you can see, this New Testament command, like the Old Testament one, deals with belief, not race.)

Surely God makes it abundantly plain that your marriage, whether to a believer or an unbeliever, is not purely a private matter. God Himself, the Church, your parents, your children, even your nation are affected.

In any other area of life you would never dream of insisting that your choices make no difference to others; for example: where you live (the neighbors have to deal with you); what kind of job you have and how you do your job (your boss and associates care); what food you eat (if you aren't healthy, your family will suffer); what friends you have (your parents or children have to put up with them); the church you choose (the whole family's spiritual health depends on your choice). Yet in such an intimate union and association as marriage, many aver that their choice of a mate is their own private concern.

Maybe you think this way. But your marriage matters to God and to me and to the bride of Christ. Your marriage matters to Christians. We are affected by it, and other young people, especially, may be influenced to follow your example in choosing an unbelieving mate. You do have a responsibility to the Church and to society to establish a stable Christian home. But above all, you must answer to God for your choice of an unbeliever who cares *nothing* for His only beloved Son.

Though it is true that we are saved souls on an individual basis, we may not adopt the destructive belief of today's society that what we do is purely our own personal affair. God has never endorsed such a laissez-faire policy. We are under His control and always in His view. In Isaiah 29:15, 16, He says, "Woe to those who deeply hide their plans from the Lord, and whose deeds are done in a dark place, and they say, 'Who sees us?' or 'Who knows us?' You turn things around!" And again: " . . . you felt secure in your wickedness and said, 'No one sees me.' Your wisdom and your knowledge, they have deluded you; for you have said in your heart, 'I am, and there is no one besides me' " (Isa. 47:10).

We reason today in this same individualistic, existential way, believing that marriage affects no one but ourselves. We must rethink the whole situation in God's perspective, from the directives of His Word. If you believe for one moment that the significance of your marriage or the significance of your sex affair outside of marriage goes no further than your bedroom, then you really haven't thought seriously enough about marriage or sex affairs.

Every culture in the world—even the most primitive, pagan, or depraved—has attached significance to the male-female relationship. They know without a doubt that the influence of such relationships extends far beyond themselves as individuals; they are aware of the effect the relationship of man and woman has on economy, government, the younger generation, and the older generation.

No, your marriage is not a strictly private matter. A host of other individuals inextricably bound to you in the name and the blood of Jesus Christ are affected or influenced, perhaps for generations to come.

3

DATING

Perhaps by now you already suspect what I intend to propose about dating, and your question is: "Well, now that you've told me not to marry an unbeliever, are you going to tell me that I should never date an unbeliever?"

Yes, I am, for I believe that the best way possible to avoid marrying an unbeliever is to avoid dating an unbeliever.

"Oh," you protest, "not all dates are *that* serious. Sometimes we date only to have a little fun and a nice evening of companionship to avoid boredom and loneliness. What's the harm in that?"

Well, we'll talk about that. But first let me tell you the usually deficient advice my generation was given about dating and marriage.

Most of the fellows girls dated then were nominal Christians—temperate, fairly honest and responsible. This was not because they loved the Lord. Nor was it because the church was sound in doctrine. It was not. But it was because our parents were coasting along morally on their forefathers' biblical principles. Rules were not obeyed because they were God's law but because it was *nice* not to lie or drink or smoke. It was *ungentlemanly* to swear and *unsportsmanlike* to cheat—not sinful. The sign of a good provider was hard work and frugality. Your image was more impressive if you refrained from working on Sunday and went to church faithfully whether you learned much about God or not—and we didn't. This was the model man the girls of my day were told to date and marry, even by most Christian parents.

I don't recall hearing any of our parents stress the fact that God commands us to marry only in the Lord. I am sure this must have been because of ignorance of God's Word. My parents were relatively new Christians. At eleven I came to know Christ as Saviour and Lord while attending evangelistic meetings in our church which was by then well along the road of liberal theology. But some truly evangelical members voted for a two-week "revival." I was fortunate enough to attend, though I went only to hear the music and singing. At this time Mother came to know Christ after years of church attendance and Dad shortly accepted Christ as Saviour after years of non-attendance. This was, I feel sure, an answer to the importunate prayers of his godly old mother.

Her memory is dear to me. I see her sitting in her favorite rocker, munching an apple and reading her Bible until her weary eyes closed. As she dozed my sister and I, perched on a stool at her feet, watched as her nodding head slowly drooped upon her chest. Curious little ones, we avidly waited for her set of upper teeth to wiggle up and down. Our muffled giggles always woke her, spoiling our fun.

This humorous, perhaps irrelevant, impression of our godly grandma pales beside the deeply etched memory of her abiding love for Christ. But, in all of her wise counsel to us, never once did *she* advise us to marry only in the Lord. Nor did my father or mother, or any other parents of Christian fellows and girls I knew stress this. Not even our pastors mentioned this command of God to us. The assumption seemed to be that we would instinctively pick the right mate. I only wish that we had had the advice of truly Reformed Christians. For the most part, the churches of our day had ceased to say that God really makes *commands*.

Well, God was good to me in spite of my lack of instruction. Somewhere, somehow, in God's grace He impressed upon me the truth in my own mind that marriage with an unbeliever could never work, that I should marry only in the Lord. I thank Him for giving me that resolve which certainly was not based on sure knowledge of God's Word. In mercy and grace He gave me a wonderful Christian husband!

It is imperative to know what God requires in marriage. I hope as I share my experience and knowledge of God's Word concerning Christian marriage I can make these truths real to your heart and then to your experience.

Back to dating. Did you know that dating is unique to our society? Only within the last century have fellows and girls had complete freedom to come and go with each other with scarcely any restrictions as to where they go, how long they stay, or whether they are alone without other couples—let alone chaperones required in other eras. Most, if not all, foreign societies realize the significance of marriage; parents select mates for their children with certain criteria in mind to make the marriage successful. The same thing was true in Bible times.

I am not advocating a return to those days, but I do think that America's dating habits should be more seriously considered, especially by Christians. What is the purpose of dating? Something to pass an evening? Or to reassure ourselves that we *are* popular? Or something young people do because of peer pressure— very young people, I mean? Is it possible to date without any effects upon us or our date? Or does dating involve really mature responsibility—to God, to ourself, to the Church, to our families, and to the one we date?

I believe that even many Christians have great difficulty seeing that dating carries great responsibility to God and to others. Our society is infused with the idea of complete individualism which isolates and insulates us from each other. We are told to look inward to find ourselves, whatever that may mean. In our preoccupation with ourselves we grow less and less concerned with others. When we Christians date, for example, our desires and the love of ourselves often are given priority over love for God and responsibility to Him and to the Church—and to the one we date. God and the Church take a second place to our egos. The problem is, of course, lack of genuine, fervent love for God based on knowledge of Him and His law.

I think of a beautiful Christian girl in her twenties who was debating whether to date a gifted fellow barely a nominal Christian. Her father and mother begged her to think seriously and prayerfully about it. Well, she thought about it briefly but decided that "just this once" would be pleasant and hurt no one.

They had a delightful evening sharing their childhood experiences (he was from a different land). All the while she thought, "I will not date him again."

But he was a persistent suitor, calling again, and again. And again and again she went with him for "just this one time," feeling that she could break it off when she wished.

Mornings found her thinking of him, and evenings she listened for his call. Time passed. The thinking and listening became a strange longing for him which defied analysis or repression. She was alarmed at how bereft she felt when not in his presence; she thought of the clasp of his hand in hers and the tender, loving gaze of his serious brown eyes.

Then he left for a business trip. Her sense of loss even greater, she thought in panic, "I must write him a letter and break this whole thing off. Oh, what could I have been thinking of? I *never* intended to become so involved. It will never work. He doesn't really know Christ."

In her anguished conviction she admitted to herself and to her parents, "He does not really have true faith in Christ." So she wrote to him.

Jolted and shaken, he returned at once and dated her more persistently and ardently than ever. She went with him, each time telling herself that in fairness she must hear him out. He finally convinced her that his unscriptural, mystical faith in Christ was as valid as hers.

It was then she knew for sure that a line had been crossed months before, a line she now lacked the will power to step back over. In fact, she didn't now want to step back over. She wanted only him. Yet she could not say just when it was she had reached the point of no return, the point where she no longer waited patiently on the Lord to speak to her so that she could have His song in her heart.

No, now she sang a different song almost against her will, it seemed to her—and yet it really wasn't against her will. God would have helped her had she asked Him sincerely. But her love for Bill overwhelmed her, surrounding and insulating her from the voice of her God, the prickles of her own conscience, and the stricken pleas of her parents, pastor and session.

The first date had turned out to be irresistible allure—enchantment and delight that seemed to speak like the very voice of God to her.

I think C. S. Lewis well explains why 'falling in love' has such powerful persuasion. In the introduction of his book *The Four Loves*[1] he says that we "may mistake Like for Same"; that is, just because "being in love" is so wonderful, it truly seems to be identical with God's love. We actually mistake it as God speaking to us. We think that the likeness to God's love makes it truly Christian love. So we give allegiance to this thing we call "being in love"; our passionate love for another may seem to be God's voice speaking to us. We think, "The Bible tells us God is love!" Lewis says we may rationalize, "If God is love, then love is God." But the Bible does not teach that.

So, the grandeur of Eros (Lewis' name for 'being in love') conceals seeds of danger because Eros speaks like a god. "His [Eros'] total commitment, his reckless disregard of happiness, his transcendence of self-regard, sound like a message from the eternal world."

This is heavy business—this being in love—with all its powerful feeling, its ennobling, self-sacrificing passion and high happiness. This alone makes it dangerous to date an unbeliever. Then there is always the trap of sexual desire. It seems so absolutely divine that we then believe we can find our absolutes in the flesh. In the heat of passionate romance we forget that spiritual absolutes and directives are not found in the flesh but in God. After all, we reason, what could possibly be wrong with such wonderful emotions and desires, especially when they are gifts from God and seem to speak to us with the very voice of God?

Well, nothing is wrong about "being in love" with the *right* person, the right person for a Christian being a *Christian*. I don't say this on my own authority. God has commanded. A Christian is to listen only to the voice of

[1]C. S. Lewis, *The Four Loves* (New York: Harcourt Brace Jovanovich, Inc., 1960), p. 19.

God. He may not listen to the voice of romantic love or to how his feelings and emotions speak when they tend to sound like the voice of God Himself. His revealed Word is the only guide.

You may start dating innocently enough, stoutly maintaining that you and your date are only friends. I've heard so many young people say this, but they forget that friendship can quickly develop into "being in love," in as little time as a half-hour, C. S. Lewis says. You cannot afford to risk the tremendous pressures of being in love with one who doesn't love Christ, for most of the time when we fall *in* love we don't want *out*.

God knows that we all need love. He has given Himself in love to us in the person of Jesus Christ. "It is not good for the man to be alone" (Gen. 2:18). So He gives us mates—and children and parents and friends and brothers and sisters. Unless all of these natural loves are under the lordship of our God they remain only natural loves given by His common grace. They are true loves, but loves unfed by the saving, supernatural love of God. These loves, Lewis says, are near to God, but it is a "nearness by likeness."[2] These loves have such splendor, joy, power, and desire for the good of our beloved; they are so God-like that we think they must be God. But we forget that all of these loves given to man are only images of God—fallen, broken, marred images of God's holy, perfect love. We still have the capacity to love because the common grace of God, given to all men, allows it to remain. But common grace is not saving grace which alone gives us true love for *God*. Though these loves given to unbelievers are real loves, they are not enduring; that is, they are not boundless in quantity or quality, because the unbeliever does not truly love God who gives eternal love to the believer. They are natural loves without the mark of eternity upon them.

Any of our loves can be consuming and addictive. We don't count the cost. We even say that anything done in the name of love is virtuous and right "as long as no one gets hurt," a very common expression today which really means that anything goes as long as we think we have done it in love.

We are on dangerous ground, indeed, when we think our natural loves are God speaking to us. We even say how close to God we feel when we are "in love." But these natural loves do not give us approach or access to God's presence. Our parents' devoted love can't knit us in union to God. Patriotic love, though something we should have, does not bring us into His presence or favor. And the sublimest natural love—*being in love*—though seemingly so God-like, does not wed us to the Bridegroom, Jesus Christ. Only

---

[2] Ibid.

our new birth and trust in the astounding, sacrificial death of our Lord Jesus for our sin does that.

As I said before, I am writing chiefly to those who have been born again by the Holy Spirit and believe in Jesus as their sin-bearer; to those who are the bride of Christ—members of His body. Hosea knew what marriage to God meant as we can see in Hosea 2:19-20: " . . . I will betroth you to Me in righteousness . . . justice . . . lovingkindness . . . compassion . . . faithfulness." His love for us is eternal and so is His righteousness, justice, lovingkindness, compassion and faithfulness embodied in His love for us. All of these attributes of God Himself become, (in less dimension, of course, because of our sin), the attributes of our earthly loves. And wonder of wonders, God promises to us, His betrothed, "Then you will know the Lord." You will know Him in a most intimate way, for Isaiah 54:5 says that our husband is our maker, whose name is the Lord of Hosts.

We believers, along with Israel, have been granted the highest privilege man can have: to *know* God; to know Him in such a loving, intimate relationship that He tells us we are His bride. What matchless love! It boggles the mind to think how close He is willing to be to us who don't deserve it at all. We are so close to God in Christ Jesus that it seems incredible we and Israel would ever be guilty of spiritual adultery. But often we are, and so was Israel. Hosea said so and God said so.

Maybe you wonder what spiritual adultery has to do with intermarriage or vice versa. Strange as it may seem, they are not so far removed from each other. You see, Israel committed spiritual adultery when they gave that honor to their idols which is due to God alone. "Ephraim, a tribe of Israel, is joined to idols . . . they have committed whoredom continually." Ephraim was *joined* to idols intimately, in love with them and addicted to them: joined to idols instead of their God. Spiritual adulterers! Unfaithful!

That was Ephraim. What does that have to do with us, God's children, today? Sad to say, we are more like Ephraim than we like to think. Ephraim betrayed their true husband because they left Him for other gods. When a Christian's love for an unbeliever comes before his love for his God,[3] he is perilously close to the idolatry of the Israelites; any dearly loved one can lead us step by senseless step down the path away from God. Samson and Solomon are proof of what half-way Christians we are capable of becom-

[3] Read the poignant, true story of a couple who made each other an idol and what happened after they became Christians: Sheldon Vanauken, *A Severe Mercy* (New York: Harper and Row, 1977).

ing when influenced by unbelieving mates. They were taken down this road away from their God by unbelieving mates.

This very thing we are talking about was then, and still is, one of the chief causes of spiritual adultery: marrying those who do not love the Lord. You see, God in His love for His bride—Old and New Testament believers—gave a law (commandment) to marry only those who have been born again.

It is usually easy for us to readily admit that lawbreaking in *other* areas always brings disaster. Defy gravity by leaping from a rooftop and you'll be seriously injured, barring a miracle; overeat and you'll suffer indigestion or worse; plant corn, but don't expect beans to grow. Most of us are not so foolish as to argue with the results of defying the rules of nature, but when it comes to spiritual rules, we do not always regard those as inviolable. We think that we can tamper a little with the laws that seem to us to be small or cramp our style. God's law to marry only in the Lord was given to us because of His love for us. He didn't give this order to spoil our love relationships but to put them in the perfect perspective of His loving plans for us. He wants us to be as perfectly, happily married as is possible on this earth. Foremost, of course, in demanding truly Christian marriage, is God's concern for His own honor and glory and the welfare of His Church. But His interest is not exclusively for Himself. He is eternally interested in *you* as a person. He cares, and He cries for you because He loves you so much. We can *grieve* His Holy Spirit by disobedience.

If you are a child of the covenant of grace, you have long been covered, literally wrapped, in the blanket of God's love. You never have really experienced His wrath. It is so easy for us when we have known the Lord from babyhood to take His love for granted. Perhaps this is why Israel so many times strayed from God and just as often brought His wrath upon themselves. When they made the golden calf to worship (Exod. 32), they probably never dreamed that God could ever be angry with *them*. *They* had *always* enjoyed His favor, hadn't they? Besides, God is a God of love, isn't He?

Well, of course He is, but we are not to presume upon that love. He cares what *you* do, how *you* treat His commands. He cares especially for the children born of *your* marriage. In another chapter we will talk about this more fully. However, I think it imperative at this point to remember God's repeated Old Testament warnings that if His people marry those who do not love God, the *godly line will be destroyed* (Deut. 7:3, 4). Destroyed because of an unbelieving parent? Doesn't this dreadful fact grip your heart in an agony of responsibility to God and to future generations of the bride of Christ?

Can we ask for a better counselor than God? Of course we can't. He is perfect and His counsel is perfect; and, like Himself, His counsel is sovereign. David said in Psalm 119 that God's testimonies were his delight; *they* were his counselors. David loved God's commandments. When the cords of wickedness encircled him, he said he did not forget God's law. If you are now dating an unbeliever, you may not consider that person to be a wicked one who encircles you because he or she seems such a nice person. Your unbelieving boyfriend or girlfriend may be considerate, kind and loving, and treat you ever so tenderly. If you don't think of him as basically wicked, as God says every unregenerate human being is, then you are not thinking deeply enough. You are not thinking of the depths of depravity of the unregenerate heart. You are seeing commendable conduct in that person—that is true. But do you know why? It is because these qualities are given to that person by the *common grace* of the Holy Spirit who restrains the wicked hearts of men so that you and others members of Christ's Church may function as believers in God's kingdom until Christ returns to earth for His own. Jesus protects His bride because she is the apple of His eye. You are a member of her body which is also the body of your Lord. This unbeliever in his present sinful state, with his propensity toward evil—with his heart unchanged by the saving operation of the Holy Spirit—is an enemy of the body of Christ, and is, therefore, really your enemy too, since you belong to Christ's body.

A person who remains *out of the Lord* cannot be joined to His body. This is the reason God has said to marry only *in the Lord*. Is this commandment your counselor? Or are you this minute involved romantically with a non-Christian fellow or girl, heedless of this counsel of God to you? Perhaps you have already reached the place of decision to marry anyway and take the consequences. The consequences, as pastors and counselors can attest, will be disastrous for you and your mate, for your children, and especially for the apple of God's eye, the Church.

God's bride, that body of believers in Jesus' saving death for sin, is the most important thing in the universe to Him. And yet, you may be saying, "My life is my own and my happiness the most important thing. As a Christian my choice of an unbelieving mate is mine alone. Am I responsible to the whole Church?" One young woman asked her parents this. Her father, an elder in the church, said, "You surely are responsible—to Christ the Head of the Church, and to every single member."

You see, what that father understood is that his believing daughter was a member, or part, of the living organism, the bride of Christ. He understood that her membership was (unlike membership in social clubs or even human families) a permanent membership. She was part of a living body which would be seriously affected by her marriage. Her father understood the law of God concerning Christian marriage. He knew that his beloved daughter was contemplating a heinous offense against the body of Christ by bringing into Christ's body a foreign member.

Here I'm reminded of present medical research in transplanting organs from one body to another. The rejection rate is high; the transplants so often don't work. And God says that in the case of marriage the taking of a sinful, foreign body and soul into union with yourself, body and soul, *never* works; not until the unbeliever's heart is supernaturally changed from a heart of stone to a heart of flesh can the two hearts of that marriage be one in thought and deed and devotion to God. And, though God is a merciful, gracious God, you may not presume upon God's saving grace to change that unbeliever when you have so wilfully made your decision to marry him.

An unbeliever does not want God's law as his counselor. Indeed, this is true of some believers also. Dr. Jay Adams cautions believers to break off dating even believers who do not want to settle problems according to God's rules.[4] Dr. Adams knows that it can be difficult and perhaps impossible to solve problems scripturally when one partner is an obedient Christian and the other a rebellious Christian. Even though both are believers, if they are divided as to how to solve problems, they will have difficulty reconciling differences and scripturally coping with their problems. Two married believers must be totally committed to Christ and His will; we are not exempt from problems just because we are Christians.

When a believer becomes deeply involved with an unbeliever or an immature, rebellious Christian, it is necessary to sacrifice that love for the sake of Christ. One girl we know did just that. Betty dated a Catholic boy. They came to care for each other deeply; he was serious enough to marry. Her Christian conscience almost too late awakened, Betty suddenly realized, as if rousing from a dream, that this was all "for real": George was *really* serious. She shook herself awake to the truth—or, rather, God did—and asked God to help her do the right thing for His sake. With

[4]Jay Adams, *Christian Living in the Home* (Phillipsburg, New Jersey: Presbyterian and Reformed Pub. Co., 1972), p. 65.

courage given only by Christ, she broke the relationship, went to another state far enough away that she and George would not see each other, and prayed for God to work things out for His own glory. God granted her request. George was born again—a miracle of God's grace—not because she had dated an unbeliever, of course. God never rewards us for evil. I truly think that God rewarded her with a new George transformed by Christ because He saw that she finally wanted His will and not her own in this matter. She did not take the attitude, as many Christian young people do when they have sinfully encouraged an unbeliever into such a close relationship, "Well, Lord, there is nothing I can do about it now. I'm going to marry, and I believe that my good Christian life may change George. Lord, you say that may happen. It's right here in I Corinthians 7:16, Lord."

If you deliberately become involved with an unbeliever and contemplate marriage, thinking that God promises to convert the unbeliever *after* marriage, then you misunderstand Paul. Paul is talking to those who were already married; he is speaking to a person who had accepted Christ as Saviour *after* marriage and then finds himself married to a mate who is still in unbelief. The case of a Christian deliberately marrying a heathen is not alluded to in the above verse. Paul was talking to those who were already married.

At that time, just as today, it happened that one of two unbelieving marriage partners became a believer; the other partner remained in unbelief. It was to the believer Paul spoke when he urged him to continue living with the unbelieving mate. God says, "How do you know, O wife, whether you will save your husband? Or how do you know, O husband, whether you will save your wife?" (I Cor. 7:16).

This hope which God holds out for the rebirth of the unbelieving mate under these conditions is a hope that we Christians may not presume upon if we have deliberately dated and finally married an unbeliever. In His great mercy, according to His own pleasure, and not because of anything we do, God may grant the conversion of an unbelieving husband or wife, but in our experience this does not seem to be the rule. We have known many Christian husbands and wives who were married for years, yet their unbelieving mates were not saved. For 50 some years one woman we knew and loved dearly prayed for her husband to come to the Lord. She admitted freely that she deliberately chose to marry him when she knew that it was wrong. She prayed. We prayed. God alone knows how many prayed for that man over the years. But he was still in unbelief when she died.

Another dear Christian woman has spent about 25 years with a man who makes all kinds of demands that compromise her Christian conscience, especially in the training of her children.

One beautiful girl who willfully chose an unbeliever has suppressed her faith to the point she cannot bring herself to teach her children the things of the Lord. Why? Because her husband's liberal views cause so much conflict. So, to keep peace, she has put into practice his beliefs instead of her own, particularly in the training of their children. It isn't difficult to see quite often the confusion and grief written upon her face.

Tragically enough, such cases in the Christian Church are more numerous than we realize. Most of these people would be the first to warn you, "Don't marry an unbeliever!"

In spite of all the warnings and pleas of concerned Christians, maybe you think even now that your deep love for your unbelieving date or fiance will work everything out for you. God says, No it won't! The husband of the girl we just mentioned thought it would. In fact, he said with great confidence that their love would find in itself the power to solve their differences as to how to train the children. But, it didn't. He did not understand that marriage can't have harmony of principles without the law and love of Christ as a basis. He did not know that his frail human love could not be full and truthful and completely honest without the source of God's love: the eternal, unfailing love of the Father which He had for us before the world was ever formed. This man did not see that without the indwelling of the Holy Spirit in the heart there is no possibility of possessing unfailing love. Not that Christians never fail to love. No. But the Christian is in possession of God's unlimited love; though he may not in every instance practice love as he should, God's love is available to him at all times upon repentance and petition for love.

The unbeliever you may plan to marry just doesn't have this kind of love for you. How can he, while his heart is a dead heart—cold as stone toward God? Any passion, any affection, any tenderness an unconverted lover may have cannot endure under the pressures of life because there is not the lasting source of God's love dwelling in the unbeliever's unregenerate heart—no indwelling of the Holy Spirit within because he has not been born again by the Spirit. All he has by way of love is what is given to him by God's common grace, in the amount God chooses to give and at the time God chooses to give it.

The unbeliever is not interested in feeding his mind on the Word of God. In his unconverted state, the voice of God is the voice of an alien to him (I Cor. 1:18; 2:14). He does not care whether he acts or feels the way God wants him to because he is not interested in pleasing Jesus Christ. So his heart is not interested in the Church or spiritual things or even his own soul, or the souls of his children.

Now we are not denying that the natural loves of the unbeliever are genuine loves. They are true loves, but they are loves given by God for His own purposes, given only to a certain point or degree and for an uncertain length of time. They are not given in inexhaustible supply as God's holy love is given to the Christian, the love spoken of by Paul: love which is patient, kind, not jealous, not arrogant, not easily provoked, forgiving wrongs suffered, rejoicing in righteousness and truth, bearing all things, hoping all things, enduring all things, never failing (I Cor. 13).

The unbeliever doesn't have *that* kind of love for you though he is ever so tender and attentive and romantic. The unbeliever can love in you what he sees to be lovable. That is easy. But he cannot love you in spite of what he sees to be unlovely. Only God can do that. And only God can give the unbeliever that kind of love through His saving grace, because God loves us like that—loves us in spite of our hatefulness and vileness.

If you are a believer you *must* have a mate with that kind of love—love that enables him to love what man by nature doesn't love. If you want your marriage partner to love you in spite of your nasty little habits and foibles, as God loves, then you must marry a believer.

Married love is like a garden. To bear beautiful blooms, the love of both partners must be motivated and fed by God's love. The saving, purifying, keeping love of God Himself must be the source of love in both husband and wife. The love of God alone can remove the weeds of discord and selfishness which are death to love's blooming.

Your marriage is most important to God, for the believer's home is the most important unit in God's Church. That is why, in deepest love for you, His child, and out of profound concern for His beloved bride, He commands you: marry *only* in the Lord.

In II Corinthians 6:17 God commands us to come away from unbelievers, not to form alliances with them. Come out, He says, from their midst and be separate and do not touch anything unclean. Imagine entering into such an intimate relationship as marriage, becoming one flesh with an unbeliever. The very thought of such an alliance should be horrifying to the one who truly loves Christ's body. We cherish our physical bodies, or as Christians we ought to: we wouldn't think of attaching anything to our bodies which would harm them. Yet many Christians think so lightly of their membership in Christ's body that they do not hesitate to marry an unbeliever.

Every action of ours which may lead to such a union—especially dating unbelievers—should be avoided. Though Paul was not dealing with dating per se, he knew what a bad effect unbelievers can have on us as they infect us with their unbelieving mores, ideas and philosophies. He tells us to conduct ourselves with wisdom toward unbelievers. Always be gracious. Speak pleasantly to them. But don't place yourself in positions of intimacy with them.

This is not to say that Christians can regard any other person as unimportant. On the contrary we are to regard all unbelievers as greatly important because they are human beings made in the image of God—fallen images, but images of worth nevertheless. Paul reminds us that we were once in the same state. Our attitude is always, "There, but for the grace of God, I would be." Our separation from unbelievers as far as real intimacy is concerned should in no wise make us contemptuous of those who do not know Christ. We must remember with deep humility that we are as undeserving as any man to be called His children. *But*, since God has covenanted with us to be *our* God, we have absolutely no right to enter into *intimate* relationships with unbelievers—particularly the most sacred, intimate union of marriage.

Another dreadful, biblical fact we *must* consider about unbelievers is that the wrath of God is on them, so we *cannot* be their intimate companions (Eph. 5:6-8). God has given His saving grace to us who believe, a gift of grace and favor not yet given to those still in unbelief. They are still (and always will be, unless God intervenes and touches their hearts) in deepest darkness; and John says if we say we have fellowship with Him and yet walk in darkness, or live with darkness, we lie and do not the truth of God. Marriage must be a unity of two persons living in the light of God. Darkness and light can never agree.

In Acts 5:14 we read that *believers* were added to the Church daily. Daily *such as were saved* (KJV), or *believers* (NASB), were added, not unbelievers. Yet many of us seem to think that it is perfectly fine with God if we bring unbelievers into His body by marrying those who are dead in sin, enemies of God having no hope of Christ's resurrection.

David speaks of the children of Israel mingling with the pagan people, people God had forbidden them to associate with. Of course, "mingling" did not then mean "dating" which was unheard of by the Israelites; as I said, dating is a fairly recent custom. Parents in Israel were accountable to God for fostering associations with pagans which would result in the giving of their sons and daughters to unbelievers (Deut. 7:2-4).

Surely Christian parents today cannot escape the clear implications of God's commands to His Church in Old Testament times. Shall we permit our covenant young people to date those outside the body of Christ, running the terrible risk of marrying them? Is the decision to date unbelievers a solely private concern of our covenant children? Shall believing children be left on their own to make such momentous decisions without the aid of parents and the spiritual guidance of the pastor and session? Can we sit by and unconcernedly see our beloved children mingle themselves in such intimate association with unbelievers—dating them, marrying them? Hosea 7:8-11 speaks of this: "Ephraim mixes himself with the nations; Ephraim has become a cake not turned [most unappetizing and worthless]. Strangers devour his strength, yet he does not know it . . . . Ephraim has become like a silly dove without sense; they call to Egypt, they go to Assyria."

Ephraim was smitten with worldly things and worldly people. It is difficult to remain separate, to place our God's wishes and will above our own. I do not for a moment minimize the pressures of today's society upon children and parents as those pressures converge upon us, trying to force us into their mold. It is difficult to fight the cult of Madison Avenue: the plethora of ads, for example, inducing us to be attractive, romantic, sexy and affluent. But we must not forget that the way of Madison Avenue is not the road to happiness and life, but (if we make that way a god) it is the road to sorrow and the very death of love. There is no real love on that road, only pagan "love."

Ezra and Nehemiah and Hosea knew this. They knew the lure of the unbelieving strangers: their grain, new wine, their glittering idols. They knew what the trouble was; Israel had left her first love, her only true God and Saviour, for the love of all that glittered and promised happiness without commitment and obedience to their God. The prophets shed tears because the people of Israel were a "holy seed." Christ was to come to earth through them. They were to keep pure and be prepared for the holy, incarnate Son of God. They were intimately related to Him, those who believed with faith in the coming Messiah. They were the most important people to God on the face of this earth. Ezra and Nehemiah kept pointing out this everlasting distinction between the saints of God and the children of this world. They saw the awful danger of the intermarriage of unbelievers with God's precious, elect children.

Our hearts should be touched by this preeminent concern of the prophets which shines through their warnings to God's people. We should see clearly that Ezra and Nehemiah were not being pigheaded or intolerant. And neither is God when in the New Testament He again gives the command: marry *only* in the Lord; " . . . do not be bound together with unbelievers" (II Cor. 6:14).

If you are now dating an unbeliever, God would have you immediately break off that relationship. You know, hard as it is to do, any love forbidden by God must be sacrificed. It isn't an easy thing to do, but neither is it impossible, except when we insist on giving in to our feelings and not giving in to God's wishes in the matter. If you permit your relationship to continue and deepen, you may find (indeed, you probably will find) that you have begun an amalgamation of spirit which is so binding, so profound, that you think it is surely from God. That is the way "being in love" feels. When your two spirits become locked together in this way, you'll find that it is nearly impossible to break off your dating. The situation is even more complicated if you have allowed yourselves to become physically involved as well. Only with the help of God can you wrench your spirits apart. And it isn't God's fault that your pain and grief are so great. It is your fault. But in such a state of affairs God always holds out hope to you. When we turn to Him in repentance He *always* gives us the help to do what's right.

Our help is in His own limitless power. With Him helping us, who of us need fail to do what we should? He loves us with incomprehensible love. Shouldn't we do all we can to requite a love like that?

4
WARNINGS AGAINST INTERMARRIAGE OF BELIEVERS TO UNBELIEVERS

Let's consider some of God's commands in the Old Testament concerning marriage.

Now perhaps you do not feel that the Old Testament has any validity as to directives for your life—let alone your marriage. But I think that we can see only too clearly that it does. Paul[1] and Jesus[2] thought so; with them we are in very good company indeed. If we stop to think that the Old Testament believers were Abraham's spiritual seed by faith, we shall see the close relationship of us with them. They were the apple of God's eye; so are we. They were called by Him and loved by Him with an everlasting love; so are we. They were members of Christ's body; so are we. God said that He was married to them, and so are we the bride of Christ.

This marriage of God to us His people should be one of our gravest considerations when contemplating dating and marriage. Listen to His tender assurance: " 'For your husband is your Maker, whose name is the Lord of Hosts; and your Redeemer is the Holy One of Israel Who is called the God of all the earth. For the Lord has called you, like a wife forsaken and grieved in spirit, even like a wife of one's youth when she is rejected,' says your God" (Isa. 54:5, 6). What a privilege and honor!

When God performed the first marriage in the Garden of Eden, Adam said, " 'This is now bone of my bones and flesh of my flesh; she shall be called Woman, because she was taken out of Man.' For this cause shall a man leave his father and his mother, and shall cleave unto his wife; and they shall be one flesh." Think of the closeness of this unique relationship of man and wife, and then think of the wonder that God Himself has entered into a relationship of spirit with us believers even closer than that of human husbands and wives.

Then why do we think it strange that God places certain restrictions upon us when He warns believers in Christ not to marry unbelievers? Hasn't He said that He wants us for Himself alone, that we must do nothing

---

[1] "The apostle Paul is so convinced of the unity which prevails between the old and new covenants that he cannot assert one of the great truths of the gospel without quoting a passage from the Old Testament for its support" (Godet, quoted by John Murray, *The Epistle to the Romans*, the New National Commentary [Grand Rapids: Eerdmans, 1968], p. 33).

[2] See Luke 21:42; 24:27 and Matthew 22:29-32.

that spiritually affects His union with us? Surely we have not thought seriously enough how union with unbelievers affects our union with God.

Suppose we look first at some of God's warnings to His people as to restrictions on intermarriage with unbelievers—Old Testament warnings first.

When Israel was about to defeat seven great nations larger and stronger than they, God told them to make no covenant with them and to show them no favor. He placed great stress upon the sin of young people marrying unbelievers, though He addressed His caution to the parents, clearly showing us parents our responsibility for our children's marriages. He said, " . . . you shall not intermarry with them; you shall not give your daughters to their sons, nor shall you take their daughters for your sons. For they will turn your sons away from following Me to serve other gods; then the anger of the Lord will be kindled against you, and He will quickly destroy you" (Deut. 7:3-4).

Surely this should cause parents to think twice before we acquiesce to any union of our believing children with unbelievers. But that is not all God said on this matter. He ordered Israel, "But thus you shall do to them: you shall tear down their altars, and smash their sacred pillars, and hew down their Asherim [thought to be a pagan wood goddess symbol], and burn their graven images with fire" (v. 5).

Why did God order what seems to us such harsh treatment? In verse 6 He tells us why: "For you are a holy people [special treasure] to the Lord your God; the Lord your God has chosen you to be a people for His own possession out of all the peoples who are on the face of the earth." (Peter tells us the same thing in I Pet. 2:9.)

God told Israel that He had not set His love on them or chosen them because they were more in number than other peoples (they were fewest in number), but because He loved them and kept His oath which He had sworn to their forefathers. He reminded them that he had brought them out of slavery to Egypt, just as Christ has brought us out of Satan's slavery.

God told them that He is faithful, that He keeps His covenant with those who love Him, but He repays with hate those who disobey Him! Therefore He said to Israel, " . . . you shall keep the commandment and the statutes and the judgments which I am commanding you today, to do them" (v. 11). He promised that if they obeyed Him He would love them and bless and multiply them.

I think it is especially significant that God said if they married believers He would bless them with children, with good crops and other prosperity, with good health, and with His constant presence. It is also significant that His blessing depended upon their obeying His command to burn the gods of these heathen nations lest they be snared by them, even the silver and gold on them. "You shall not," God said, "bring an abomination into your house . . .; you shall utterly detest it and you shall utterly abhor it . . ." (v. 26).

Surely we can infer from this order to God's chosen people that we, His chosen ones today, are not to become intimately attached to unbelievers or to their false Jesuses or beliefs.

Why is this? We are a holy people, set apart for God Himself. God makes this clear in both the Old and New Testaments many times. In Exodus 19:6 God reminds Israel, " . . . and you shall be to Me a kingdom of priests and a holy nation." As we said before, Peter tells us this applies to all believers in Christ. God tells *us* that if we keep His covenant, then we shall be His own possession among all peoples. We belong to His kingdom.

To keep God's covenant requires conscious effort and diligence on our part. Promises are hard for humans to keep. Almost before we realize it our emotions can draw our thoughts away from God, and then we act as our feelings direct and not as God commands. This is so true in unchristian man and woman relationships. God knows that very quickly worship of Himself may be supplanted by worship of another person who has another God. In Exodus 34:12-16 God again reminds His people to make no covenant with the inhabitants of the land into which they were going, lest such a covenant become a trap—a trap because these people bowed down to idols.

" . . . for you shall not worship any other god, for the Lord whose name is Jealous, is a jealous God . . ." (v. 14). Tear down their altars, he told Israel, lest you make a covenant with them and play the harlot with their gods. You see, God has a holy jealousy, as different from our sinful jealousy as day from night or good from evil—a holy jealousy which desires to preserve His honor and glory and the loyalty of our devotion to Him as our Husband. And He knows that though we may desire to serve Him only, an attraction to an unbelieving partner will profoundly affect our worship of Him. Indeed, He makes it very clear that an unbelieving husband or wife will surely lead one away from God, and that is sin. The worship of other gods He calls harlotry, or spiritual adultery—unfaithfulness to God our Husband. And very often this unfaithfulness to God leads to unfaithfulness to our earthly mates. In fact, unfaithfulness to God always leads to many other sins as well.

In Exodus 34:15 God seems to indicate that the trouble of spiritual adultery starts first with making a covenant with the pagans, fraternizing with them (perhaps we would call it "dating" today). Then, he says, you "play the harlot with their gods," and "someone invites you to eat of his sacrifice." And then, He continues, "you take some of his daughters for your sons, and his daughters play the harlot with their gods, and cause your sons also to play the harlot with their gods" (v. 16).

In almost all marriages of believers to unbelievers this is the natural progression: downward, away from the true God. This happens almost without exception. God didn't give us these warnings for nothing. He *knows* exactly what happens when His law is ignored. Job asks the pertinent question: "Who has defied God without harm?" The answer is, of course, No one.

In Joshua's farewell address to Israel, he brought God's Word cautioning the people to cling to the Lord their God. He reminded them of their unique position as God's possession, of all that God had done for them. " . . . take diligent heed to yourselves, Joshua said, "to love the Lord your God." And once more stressing the dangers of intermarriage with unbelievers, God, through Joshua, said, "For if you ever go back and cling to the rest of these nations, these which remain among you, and intermarry with them, so that you associate with them and they with you, know with certainty that the Lord your God will not continue to drive these nations out from before you; but they shall be a snare and a trap to you, and a whip on your sides and thorns in your eyes, until you perish from off this good land which the Lord your God has given you" (Josh. 23:12, 13). God held out no hope to them that their marriages would be happy.

All of God's warnings are given to us not to cause us pain and spoil our fun but because He loves us more than any other person could ever love us. He warns so that we will not do anything to dilute our love and obedience to Him. And He *is* concerned with our happiness, even though we don't deserve it and many times think He isn't concerned. In the New Testament the same admonishments for God's children to be holy and separated from the world continue.

In His high priestly prayer (John 17), Jesus prayed for his disciples, "I do not ask Thee to take them out of the world, but to keep them from the evil one. They are not of the world, even as I am not of the world. Sanctify them in the truth; Thy word is truth."

Then Jesus prayed for all of us who believe that He died for our sin:

> I do not ask in behalf of these alone [the disciples], but for those also who believe in Me through their word; that they may all be one; even

> as Thou, Father, art in Me and I in Thee, that they also may be in Us; that the world may believe that Thou didst send Me. And the glory that Thou has given Me I have given to them . . . and Thou in Me, that they may be perfected in unity, and the world may know that Thou didst love Me . . . . Father, I desire that they also, whom Thou has given Me, be with Me where I am, in order that they may behold My glory . . . (vv. 20-24).

Think a moment in wonder about that statement of Jesus that we are loved by the Father with the same love He has for His Son. And notice that Jesus prayed that we might be kept pure, sanctified, made holy for Himself.

Paul, in II Corinthians 6:14-18, stresses this same idea of the set-apart-in-holiness believer. In verse 14 he commands, "Do not be bound together with unbelievers; for what partnership have righteousness and lawlessness, or what fellowship has light with darkness?" Paul makes it clear that God does not want us to be mismated with unbelievers. Phillips' translation reads:

> Don't link up with unbelievers and try to work with them. What common interest can there be between goodness and evil? How can there be harmony between Christ and the devil? What can a believer have in common with an unbeliever? What common ground can idols hold with the temple of God? For we, remember, are ourselves living temples of the living God. (vv. 14-16).

Paul refers us to what God Himself has said about our separateness and holiness:

> I will dwell in them and walk in them . . . . and be ye separate, saith the Lord, And touch no unclean thing; And I will receive you, And will be to you a Father, And ye shall be to me sons and daughters, Saith the Lord Almighty (vv. 16-18).

Paul goes on, "With these promises ringing in our ears, dear friends, let us keep clear of anything that smirches body or soul. Let us prove our reverence for God by consecrating ourselves to him completely" (I Cor. 7:1, Phillips).

In his letter to the Ephesians, chapter 5, Paul said that no impure or immoral person or any idolater has an inheritance in the kingdom of Christ. "Let no one deceive you with empty words, for because of these things the wrath of God comes upon the sons of disobedience. Therefore do not be partakers with them" (vv. 6-7). Here, I believe, Paul is speaking of being the close companion of unbelievers.

Paul calls to the Ephesians' attention that they "were formerly darkness, but now you are light in the Lord; walk as children of light . . . trying to learn what is pleasing to the Lord. And do not participate in the unfruitful deeds of darkness, but instead even expose them; for it is disgraceful even to speak of the things which are done by them in secret" (vv. 8-12).

So, if God does not want us to be close companions with unbelievers, nor to participate in their deeds, how can we ever imagine that He would bless the marriage of one of his own children to an unbeliever? Marriage is an even closer relationship than the ones Paul warns us about in these verses.

Furthermore, we believers are members of the body of Christ and our bodies are the temples of God, Paul points out. The Holy Spirit lives within us. We are to present our bodies to God as living sacrifices to Him because we love Him. We may not use these temples of the living God in any way we choose, but only as God has directed us.

Friendship with the world, says James, is hostility toward God. "Therefore whoever wishes to be a friend of the world makes himself an enemy of God" (James 4:4). In verse 5 we are told that God jealously desires the Spirit which He has made to dwell in us. We grieve[3] God the Holy Spirit by friendship with the world.

The intimate relationship of marriage is a great deal more than just friendship. If the Holy Spirit is grieved by our unholy friendships, then just think how saddened He is if we become one flesh with an unbeliever.

Malachi was the last prophet to Israel in the Old Testament. He tells Israel that John the Baptist is the next prophet who will announce Jesus as the Messiah. But before he tells them that, he rebukes them for two great sins they practice at this time: (1) taking strange wives of heathen nations; (2) divorce of the first wife to marry a second. God accuses them of profaning the holy covenant He had made with them. (Today, I think it is largely forgotten that marriage is a contract and covenant with God as well as with each other.)

The Israelites were His special people, recipients of the grace of the triune God of the universe. Yet by these and other despicable acts, they showed contempt for Him. This mingling with unbelievers violated the ancient, authoritative covenant contracted by God with their forefathers. God reminded them that they were one body. He had cared for their physical needs and has given them spiritual life peculiar and antithetical to the

[3]Ephesians 4:30: "And do not grieve the Holy Spirit of God, by whom you were sealed for the day of redemption." Many things beside an unchristian marriage grieve the Spirit: bitterness, anger, malice, love of material things, deception, hypocrisy, and more. But we are specifically concerned with the grief of bad marriages for now.

idolatrous spirit of those in other nations. Israel was "holy unto the Lord," set apart for God's glory. This singular distinction became lightly thought of by Israel. Instead of maintaining devotion to God, seeking to keep their status as His beloved by obeying His command to marry only believers, they married daughters of a strange nation. The great harm was not in the fact that these women were daughters of another nation or race (God is the Creator of all men), but the harm was in the fact that they were worshipers of a false god—unbelievers.

Israel's rebellion was hateful and grievous to their God who had bestowed His highest honors upon them, giving them freely His eternal, husbandly love. Many times He called it an abominable thing for those who profess to be holy in the Lord to profane that holiness by yoking themselves to unbelievers.

I do hope that the above accounts do not by now have you saying, Ho hum! Just before His warnings in Malachi, God rebuked the Israelites for saying ho hum because they were weary of hearing Him and serving Him: "You also say, 'My, how tiresome it is!' And you disdainfully sniff at it," says the Lord of hosts, "and you bring what was taken by robbery, and what is lame or sick; so you bring the offering! Should I receive that from your hand?"

You see, they were really sniffing their noses at God's requirements for His Church. They were sick and tired of His orders, of the details involved, like selecting the best sheep for sacrifice.

Perhaps you feel that the Israelites couldn't help but be bored. They were only human, weren't they? Well, if we react that way we had better ask ourselves whether it was boredom, with which we can sympathize, perhaps, or whether it was hostility. God knew they were more than just bored, I think. They sniffed at serving Him, He said. At heart they were still rebels against God.

Maybe by now you are also bored by repetition of God's command to marry only in the Lord. But repetition still is the best way to learn. Jesus said we are His little children, and, to enter the kingdom, we must be like little children. Little children do not mind repetition—they seem to love it. They are not usually bored by it; they are trusting and open and readily taught. Like the Israelites, we Christians need to hear God speak His commands and His promises again and again. That's the only way we learn; and, like children, we are prone to forget His orders.

Even much repetition didn't always help Israel, nor will it help us if, like Israel, we won't listen. We must ask the Lord to *make* us easily taught. To be easily taught does not mean that we are naive, gullible, dumb or ignorant. Christians should easily learn of God because they completely trust everything He says. If we really love Him and trust His wise rule over us, we'll have no difficulty learning whom we should marry: that one He has chosen for us from all eternity. I pray that God will enable you to do this.

5
YOUR MARRIAGE STRENGTHENS OR WEAKENS YOUR HOME

The first institution created by God was the home. It is the most important thing on earth to Him because He covenants with Christian *parents* to be *their* God and the God of *their children*. The Church is composed of the parents and children of Christian homes. God's covenant was first with believers in the nation of Israel, then with Christian believers of New Testament times, or the New Covenant times, we could say. Children trained in the Lord in New Testament Christian homes and children trained in believing Israelitish homes (if they had, or have, saving faith in Christ) are the seed of Abraham. They are a spiritual seed, if gentiles, and both spiritual and physical seed of Abraham, if converted Jews.

No institution is more sacred, more precious to God than the Christian home. The Christian home is the Church, and the Church consists primarily of Christian homes—believing parents and their covenant children. What affects one affects the other because in general God works out His plans through His covenant with Christian parents to be their God and the God of their children. Of course, we see exceptions made in God's electing grace; many who have no earthly family are born into the family of God by the Holy Spirit; too, God calls many into His fold who have been totally unacquainted with the gospel as well as many who have been trained in false religions. But for the most part God works in covenant with Christian parents and calls out whole families to be the building blocks of His Church. All of us who are born into the family of God by the new birth and have faith in Jesus Christ are equal in His sight and are living stones in His Church.

Suppose we first talk a bit about the positive aspects of a truly Christian marriage. Since God is the author of marriage and our final authority on marriage, perhaps it will be well to start with that first marriage by God in the Garden of Eden (Gen. 2:22-25). God saw that it was not good for man to be alone. He needed a mate suitable to be his helper, a wife who would so complement Adam that both of them would contribute to each other physical joy, mental and emotional stamina and spiritual strength. Eve was the woman God made, the suitable mate and Adam's equal under God. Adam was submissive to God and Eve was to be submissive to Adam. She was to be joined to Adam physically and spiritually; what God had joined no man was ever to separate (this holds true for unbelievers too, even though they may not acknowledge it).

The marriage of Adam and Eve was a covenant consecrated in the name of God—God the Father, God the Son, and God the Holy Spirit, one God. Just so, the marriage of two Christians is a covenant with God.

God dwells in the Christian home of two believers. He lives and fellowships with us. This is our highest privilege and joy: to love and to be loved by Him. Indeed, the Christian home is the Church in microcosm, we might say, because where two or three are gathered together in His name, there the invisible Church exists with Christ in their midst. Husband and wife are entrusted by God with the privilege and responsibility of establishing and caring for this most important institution on earth, the home. It often has been said that as our homes go, so go the Church, the schools, and the nation.

The home without Christ as the Head is not a truly happy, integrated home. "Except the Lord build the house, they labor in vain who build it . . ." (Ps. 127:1). In the Christian home with two individuals one in Christ, there is harmony, oneness of spirit, and the presence of Christ Himself. Parents are one in body, spirit and commitment to Christ. The living God makes them one. Yet it requires much thought, effort, and prayer on the part of both husband and wife to become more and more united in Christ.

The roles of both parents must be clearly defined, understood, and followed. In such a Christian relationship the deepest needs of a man and woman and their children are supplied. The mutual sharing and sacrificial giving of self to each other, the practice of truthful communication, the worship of their mutual Saviour, build and restore to make them more like Christ. Christian partners help each other to grow and mature to Christ-likeness, the thing for which we are created, the very purpose of our new birth into God's family (Rom. 8:29).

As in every other institution there must be structure and order, so God has ordained the husband to be the loving head (not boss or dictator) whose authority is to be so much like Christ's authority over the Church that a wife gladly and willingly submits. This submission is no threat at all to a wife's identity or freedom. She knows who she is as Christ's own child and what her worth is as Christ's own creation and possession. She knows that she is cherished by her husband as Christ cherishes the Church. She is perfectly free to do the things God wants her to do, to use her talents fully for His sake and His glory. She is equal to her husband in Christ—equal but different, with responsibilities no less important than her husband's.

She is one with her husband; indeed, a mysterious fusion and amalgamation of body and soul take place so that wife and husband are one. She is her husband; her husband is herself. They are one in flesh and one in spirit, if both are Christians. Their separate identities remain intact; yet as long as they live on this earth they are one as Christ and the Church are one, indissolubly bound with no possible way for disunion or separation.[1]

Over the years, with Christ the Head of their home, husband and wife should become more and more one in the Lord. In this kind of union, if communication in truth with each other is good, every aspect of their life together will become more and more satisfying. This oneness of body, soul, and spirit in the Lord gives meaning and dimension to all of life in marriage: sex, child-rearing and development, worship, recreation, education, work, budgeting, development of talents, community and church work—all activity.

We can touch only briefly upon the positively Christian marriage[2] because in this book our concern is for the marriage not positively Christian, the marriage with one partner Christian, the other partner unbelieving. We are concerned with the effects of such mixed marriages upon parents, the children, and the Church.

Unbelief and belief are as foreign to each other as good is to evil. Indeed, one *is* good, the other, evil. Amos realized this when he asked, "Can two walk together, except they be agreed?" (Amos 3:3, KJV). Or play together? live together? sleep together? we might ask. Paul asked in II Corinthians 6:15 and 16, ". . . what harmony has Christ with Belial, or what has a believer in common with an unbeliever?" He told the Corinthians not to be bound together (unequally yoked) with unbelievers because righteousness and lawlessness or light and darkness can have no real fellowship. It is impossible. He goes on to say that the temple of God (the Christian) can have no agreement with idols.

Calvin said that when Paul spoke of having "nothing in common" he was not referring to food, clothing, sun and rain, but to the "special properties" believers have which unbelievers do not have, namely Christ and His truth. Lenski, in the *Interpretation of I and II Corinthians* (p. 188), says the unbeliever's yoke is principally his unbelief: "The unbeliever would laugh

---

[1] God grants that three things may dissolve a marriage: (1) death, (2) wilful desertion, (3) adultery.

[2] No Christian couple reaches the perfectly ideal marriage; but that doesn't excuse us from working hard to attain the best marriage we can under Christ.

at the suggestion of his taking on faith's yoke; yet, instead of scorning unbelief's yoke many a believer accepts it upon his neck and even imagines that he can still retain faith's yoke." What in the world is the Christian doing, helping an unbeliever by wearing his yoke? It will break your neck, Paul seems to say—all the little unbeliefs as well as the big ones.

Joshua warned Israel that intermarriage with unbelievers would cause them nothing but trouble: "For if you ever go back and cling to the rest of these nations, these which remain among you, and intermarry with them, so that you associate with them and they with you, know with certainty that the Lord your God will not continue to drive these nations out from before you; but they shall be a snare and a trap to you, and a whip on your sides and thorns in your eyes, until you perish from off this good land which the Lord your God has given you" (Josh. 23:12, 13). The believer's life is obedience to law; the unbeliever's life is lawlessness. Such lawlessness, like thorns in the eyes, can bring only sorrow and tears to the believer, and like whips on the sides, hurt and anguish. The Holy Spirit within the believer is hurt and grieved by the scorn and contempt the unbeliever holds for the law of God. Belial (Satan) and Christ never agree. Darkness drives away light.

In the above verses from Joshua, God gave the Israelites no hope of having harmony in marriage to unbelievers. Until you perish, he said, they shall be nothing but trouble and heartache to you.

Occasionally, for reasons of His own, out of mere undeserved favor—perhaps in answer to prayers of God's people—God does set an unequally yoked marriage straight. The unbeliever may become a believer, but honest observation of such marriages forces us to see that a deliberately planned union in defiance of what a Christian knows to be his plain orders from God usually limps along for years in an undivided state. I asked three pastors if they knew of any unbeliever who became a Christian after a wilfully contracted mixed marriage. They all thought carefully and then answered that as far as they could remember they never had known of one.

We personally knew two believing wives who after 50 years of marriage never saw their husbands come to know Christ. They struggled alone for years, trying singlehandedly to train their children in the Lord. We see any number of young and middle-aged men and women in the same heartbreaking struggle against the brick wall of unbelief in their husbands and wives. Often the battle becomes intolerable for them. They give up, coming more and more under the influence of their unbelieving partners, failing their children, the Church, God, and themselves.

I think of the story told about Mark Twain's wife, supposedly a true story. It has a good lesson for us. An atheist, Mark Twain married a woman who loved Jesus Christ. All through the years his atheism gradually affected her faith. When she was ill and dying, she begged him to help her. He replied by directing her to rely on her own faith. She looked searchingly at him, pathetically admitting that her faith was gone, eroded and vitiated by her close union to him.

And that's the way it always works, unless God in mercy and love, out of His own good pleasure, chooses to intervene in the heart of the unbeliever. We have no right to presume, to suppose that He will give the unbeliever a new heart of belief if we have rebelled deliberately against His command to marry only in the Lord. As we said in "Dating" (p. 24), you may not plead I Corinthians 7:16. This verse applies to one who becomes a believer in a marriage contracted by *two unbelievers*. Then God gives the new, believing partner hope that his or her unbelieving partner will come to know Christ as Savior. (Please understand, we are not saying that unbelieving partners of wilfully contracted mixed marriages *never* become believers. In God's grace there is that possibility if He wills it; God is a merciful, compassionate God. We do not *presume* upon His mercy, that's all.)

In the chapter on dating we talked about the impossibility of the union of a nonspiritual (unsaved) person to a spiritual (saved) person. This union of foreign spirits may be illustrated by the present-day attempts to transplant the heart of one person into another's body. The incidence of rejection is high—the greatest problem, in fact. The body of the recipient is caused much pain, and the donated part has burdens imposed upon it which it cannot endure, burdens which are foreign to its nature. There is discord and war between the body and the new member which, out of its own element, cannot function as God intended. As all analogies break down somewhere, so does this one, but I believe it serves forcefully to show us some truths about efforts of a believer to achieve real union in any area of marriage to an unbeliever.

The believer is of the kingdom of God. The Holy Spirit indwells him (or *her*—I don't want to seem guilty of chauvinism!). The believer has a new nature; he is born again—born into the family of God; he is God's adopted child, Paul says. The unbeliever is still, as Jesus told the Pharisees, a child of Satan, under his control, with his unbelieving nature operating to some extent in every work he does, no matter how worthy his works may be. Belief and unbelief cannot be friends, only enemies diametrically opposed to each other. In a mixed marriage you eat with, make decisions with, go to bed with an enemy—your enemy and God's enemy. This leads to endless arguments and frustration to both husband and wife. No marriage can endure such strain and friction for long. Rejection, partial or complete, is inevitable. The unbeliever (the transplanted member), placed in an environment foreign to his sinful nature, has all kinds of mental sresses and emotional strains imposed upon him because he views everything in marriage from a different perspective than his believing mate: the problems of child raising, discipline, finances, amusements, religious education. Everything is solved according to a philosophy usually opposed to Christian principles, unless the believer is strong enough and aggressive enough always to insist on biblical decisions. That causes friction.

To be strong and righteously aggressive is difficult for a believer who has already compromised enough to marry an unbeliever. By contracting such a marriage the believer has already shown that his will has been influenced by the unbeliever; he is already in a compromised situation which makes him appear weak and wavering in principle and resolve. The unbeliever appears to be the stronger of the two; indeed, he is the stronger, for he has not changed his mind at all in his stand against the truth. The believing mate has exposed himself to doubt and mistrust on the part of the children and the unbelieving mate. They well may ask him: "How much does your faith in Christ *really* mean to you, anyway, that you would so violate it?"

If the believing mate is the wife and mother and she sincerely desires the children to be trained in the Lord as God has commanded, then she must assume the spiritual leadership of the home; she suffers strain for taking the role of headship in the home, a role which is not rightfully hers, but a role which her unbelieving husband is incompetent and unwilling to undertake. He cannot teach his children how to know and love God. How can he when he himself doesn't know and love Him?

A mixed marriage can be only a superficial union because only Christ can give it true unity in body and spirit. Unbelief and belief are as antithetical as good and evil. They will not mix or agree. They reject each other 100 percent. It is highly unfair to an unbeliever for a Christian to deliberately involve him in such a sinful alliance, an explosive situation highly charged with positive and negative attitudes, motives and desires. Matthew Henry said, ". . . those who are ill-matched are already half ruined." Though he said that over three hundred years ago, it is as true today as then.

So from the very outset a mixed marriage is a divided one. The believer has already shown willingness to compromise his faith—a dreadful sign of weakness. He has, from the moment of agreement to marry (even in his agreement to date) the unbeliever, suffered loss of faith and credibility on the part of his unbelieving partner.

This division and compromise will affect every area of the couple's married life. It will affect them socially. What about friends? Usually the unbeliever cannot stand the Christian friends of his believing mate. Their interests are not his. He is irritated and bored by their talk, their goals, and their lives. The Christian's ideas of amusements, recreation, and social times are idiotic to him. Nightclubs and church picnics, for example, have little in common. Horse racing and betting are opposed to good stewardship of one's time and money. The keeping of the Sabbath day, involving worship and works of mercy and necessity for the believer, means little to the unbeliever except as an extra day to do as *he* pleases, not as God pleases. The Christian work ethic holds meaning for him only when it serves his advancement. When it doesn't, he may employ unethical, unchristian or even criminal acts to promote his prosperity—motives his Christian mate finds abhorrent. Child training from the non-Christian's point of view is in most ways opposed to the Christian's imperatives from God to train children in the Lord. The unbeliever trains them out of the Lord, away from the Lord.

The friction and irritation engendered by such constant effort and disagreement in decision making are shattering to the spiritual welfare of the believer and to the emotional well-being of both mates. Such strain is energy depleting and debilitating to both Christian and non-Christian. These day by day prosaic cares and practical problems of living—decision making by two minds opposed in belief—are what distract a couple and take them away from God and what He wants for their lives. Even for two married Christians who agree to God's standards, decision making is not always easy; but at least it is not an impossible task for them, since they love Christ and have a base for arriving at amicable conclusions, namely God's Word. Usually an unbeliever acts according to what he wants; if he acts in agreement with his believing mate it is usually because he gives in to please his mate, not because he wants to please God. He is not concerned with what God wants; indeed, it is unfair of his Christian mate to expect him to care what God wants. He really can't care about God's will because of his fallen nature. He does what comes naturally to him, making decisions which please his fallen nature.

'Self' is no doubt the biggest obstacle to overcome in any marriage (Christian or not), and 'self' is what the unbeliever has in abundance because it has not been nailed to the cross of Christ. Those of us who have been redeemed by Christ can surely vouch that it was self-pride that kept us from caring about God, from coming to Him. God had to change our inmost being, our hearts, so we could see Christ as Saviour and Lord. We are unknown to ourselves. Jeremiah tells us, chapter 17:9, "The heart is more deceitful than all else and is desperately sick; who can understand?" God goes on to say, "I the Lord search the heart, I test the mind, even to give to each man according to his ways, according to the results of his deeds" (v. 10).

Only God sees and understands the depravity of the heart:

> But to the wicked God says,
> "What right have you to tell of My statutes,
> And to take My covenant in your mouth?
> "For you hate discipline,
> And you cast My words behind you . . . .
> And you associate with adulterers.
> "You let your mouth loose in evil,
> And your tongue frames deceit.
> "You sit and speak against your brother;
> You slander your own mother's son.
> "These things you have done, and I kept silence;
> You thought that I was just like you;
> I will reprove you, and state the case in order
> before your eyes."[3]

David was aware of the deceitfulness of his own heart. In Psalm 51:5 he says, "Behold, I was brought forth in iniquity, and in sin my mother conceived me." In Psalm 58:3 he declares, "The wicked are estranged from the womb; these who speak lies go astray from birth." David said these things after his heinous crime against Uriah, his faithful captain, whose wife David took for his own after he had Uriah killed at the front in battle.

David must have been astonished that he himself, so blessed and beloved of God, could have fallen so low. This is true of any of us as Christians who have given in to the baseness which remains within us, but we do have power over sin through Jesus Christ, a power of the indwelling Holy Spirit who is greater than any remnants of self within us. The unbeliever has more than just remnants of sin to deal with and yet has no power but his own; he is left all alone to deal with his unregenerate fallen self, sustained only by

[3]See Psalm 50:16-21.

that measure of common grace God deigns to give him. And his mate and children are left to deal with all the manifestations of his fallen nature: self-love, self-pity, self-will, self-assertion, self-centeredness, self-complacency, self-aggrandizement, self-delusions, self-interest, self-deceit—the list is endless.

Putting self first—the natural, nearly constant tendency of every heart not born again—reverses the order of God's whole scheme for the home. It disturbs the peace and harmony of worship, work, play, companionship, and every other relationship. Engendered between Christian and unbeliever is abiding friction which erodes and destroys. Why? The hard answer is: The Christian is married to an enemy of God. The unchristian partner is an enemy of the Church of Christ, just as Paul was before his new birth. He is an enemy of the believing mate's soul and of the souls of his own children, for he is not the slightest bit interested in the salvation of his children's souls. He is uninterested in the gospel; it is "foolishness" to him, the Bible says: "But the natural man does not accept the things of the Spirit of God; for they are foolishness to him, and he cannot understand them, because they are spiritually appraised" (I Cor. 2:14).

The unbeliever is dead[4] in trespasses and sin; he cannot respond to the loving invitation of Christ until the Holy Spirit opens his heart to His Word.

I believe we do not consider often enough this awful fact of the enmity toward God in the heart not born again. When you marry an unbeliever you dwell with God's enemy; you go to bed with your Saviour's enemy; you eat with him, make plans with him, play with him, dwell in the closest fellowship of all with him—striving, seeking to wed together a divided home. Jesus says this can't possibly be done: a house divided against itself cannot stand (Luke 11:17).

David knew what it was like to live in a divided house and so did his son Solomon. David did wrong in multiplying his heathen wives. The sons of the marriages disturbed the peace of his home and of his kingdom. Adonijah, David's son by Haggith, was beautiful, spoiled, and cared nothing for God. He not only desired to marry his father's beautiful young wife, Abishag, but coveted David's throne as well. He begged Solomon's mother, Bathsheba, to speak to Solomon in his behalf: "Please speak to Solomon the king, for he will not refuse you, that he may give me Abishag the Shunammite as a wife."[5] Bathsheba, who, it seems to me, showed

[4]See Ephesians 2:1.

[5]I Kings 2:17; see verses 13-25.

unconcern for doing the right thing, honored his request. But Solomon, who felt that this request was an insidious claim to the kingdom had Adonijah, his half brother, put to death.

Though we can't attribute the staggering, unbelievable acts of conspiracy, deceit, violence, and crime in David's family entirely to David's marriages, we can be sure that his marriages certainly gave rise to many grave problems. Of course, there were other factors: David's own bad examples of lust and violence; his doting, preferential treatment of Amnon and Absolom; his failure to discipline his children. Certainly his heathen wives failed to help him raise the covenant children of that home in the nurture and admonition of the Lord as they should have done. They were not helpers "meet" (that is, suitable) for David as God said a man's helper must be; David should have had only one wife—a believing one.

In all fairness we must mention that David wholeheartedly repented of his sin; he is called a man after God's own heart. God forgave him. This gives all believers hope. Though David sinned in marrying enemies of the only true God, God in His mercy and sovereignty brought good out of evil. This does not mean that we can deliberately flout God's law with the notion in the back of our mind that He will bring about good. No, we Christians are subject to the will of Him, our triune God, who desires our well-being and highest good. When we seek His will in every area of life, our well-being is assured, even in trials or disaster. When we marry, His commands are to be obeyed. God tells us that we are His friends in Christ. Because we are His friends we may never marry His enemies. An enemy of God partakes of a different cup than does a believer in Jesus Christ. God draws the line very finely between the two cups (I Cor. 10:21). The believer cannot drink of the cup of the Lord and the cup of demons at the same time, for one cup is filled with the goodness of God and the other with the poison of evil. In the marriage of believer to unbeliever this dichotomy, this division of good and evil, permeates every area of married life. It *never* changes unless God chooses to change the heart of the unbeliever to a believing heart which drinks of the same cup of God's love.

Now I know that it is a most difficult thing to think of one you dearly love as an enemy of God. Jesus said, though, that we would have enemies in our own household. Sometimes we have unbelieving children or in-laws or parents in a Christian home. But the most intolerable situation is to have a *mate* who is our enemy because he does not love our God. Jesus may have had this most intimate situation in mind when He spoke the words, " . . . and a man's enemies will be members of his household" (Matt. 10:36).

An enemy of God by his very nature comes between us and God. C. S. Lewis says that it is sometimes necessary to disqualify our nearest and dearest when they come between us and our obedience to God. Jesus said, "If anyone comes to Me, and does not hate his own father and mother and wife and children and brothers and sisters, yes, even his own life, he cannot be My disciple" (Luke 14:26). He meant that we are to hate anyone who comes before Him in our devotion. It does seem like hate to the one we disqualify. Yet, you may protest, Jesus says that we are to *love* our *enemies*. Jesus is not contradicting Himself; He is only asking us to place our priority of love for Him above all other loves. Then we are able to love with Christ's love those who come between us and Christ, though at the same time hating their sin.

Loving Christ above all others is a divine gift of love. The gift of God's love enables us to love what is not lovable. This is impossible for the unbeliever. He may show love as long as we love him, but let him detect one iota of ugliness or avarice or any other vice in us and he cannot find it in himself to love us in spite of these flaws. He may overlook them or ignore them, but he cannot forgive them with God's love because he does not possess the true forgiving love of God. He has never experienced true forgiveness because of God's love. It is alien to his unregenerate nature. Jesus pointed this out—this failure to love at all times no matter what—when He asked about loving those who misuse you. Constant love is difficult even for Christians, but it is impossible for unbelievers. The power to love even your enemies must come from Christ. A truly happy marriage cannot exist without this unique divine love in both mates.

In the Old Testament, God told the Israelites that their enemies, the heathen who hated God, would strip Israel of their clothing and their jewels. The beautiful clothing and jewels God had given them Israel misused to adorn their idol temples and groves and high places. The clothing was fine, delicate clothing. The jewels, beautiful. God had given them the very best. Yet they turned their jewels into idols! One of their worst sins was the sacrifice of their own children to idols; God said they were *His* children, the "sons and daughters whom you had borne to Me" (Ezek. 16:20). They were murdered in the name of an idol. God asked whether this is a small matter.

As I read this account my heart breaks at the tragedy of Christian young people we have known who have been stripped of their matchless robes of faith (or at least had them badly tattered); who have abandoned the jewels of grace to fraternize with idols; who have sacrificed their covenant children to the barren desert and cold winds of unbelief in an unchristian mate. And God still asks, "Is this a small matter?"

Israel, the covenant people of God, had entered into leagues and alliances with Egypt. God called this spiritual adultery because He had betrothed Himself to them as their only Husband, and they had left Him for other gods, the gods of these heathen people. Those whom the Israelites found so attractive and irresistible were in reality their enemies who did not love them—who actually hated them. These Israelites whom God loved with everlasting love had actually betrothed themselves to their spiritual enemies; God called them covenant breakers (Ezek. 16:59). God was jealous with a perfectly holy jealousy of Israel's strange loves, and He is jealous when a Christian betrays His love by marrying an unbeliever.

So much is said only of God's love today that it is very difficult for us to really believe God when He says that His wrath is on unbelievers, particularly when they seem to be such kind, loving, thoughtful people. But God tells us the truth about ourselves and our relationship to Him before we are born again by His Holy Spirit. In Ephesians 5:5-9 He again clearly draws the line of demarcation between unbeliever and believer: "For this you know with certainty, that no immoral or impure person or covetous man, who is an idolater, has an inheritance in the kingdom of Christ and God. Let no one deceive you with empty words, for because of these things the wrath of God comes upon the sons of disobedience. *Therefore do not be partakers with them; for you were formerly darkness, but now you are light in the Lord; walk as children of light (for the fruit of the light consists in all goodness and righteousness and truth)* . . . ."[6] "Do not," God continues, "participate in the unfruitful deeds of darkness, but instead even expose them . . ." (v. 11).

God's special favor is upon the Christian believer and His wrath is upon unbelievers, so we cannot be their intimate companions. This favor to be His own intimate children is one not yet bestowed upon those still in unbelief. They are in deep spiritual darkness. If we say we have fellowship with Him and yet walk in darkness or live with darkness, we lie and do not practice truth (I John 1:6). If Christian marriage should reflect anything, it should reflect truth—the daily practice of truth in love and in communication. This dealing with each other in truth is the very essence of marriage; truth makes us really one, because Christ is the Truth.

---

[6]Italics mine.

This oneness is difficult to achieve even for two married believers committed to God's truth, but it is an impossible thing to attain for a believer married to an unbeliever. In such a marriage the Christian cannot fully express how he feels or what he believes or thinks. Neither can the unbeliever. Truth and falsehood constantly collide. Neither mate can be truly honest without hurting the other because of this basic, ever present dichotomy of beliefs. The Christian and the unbeliever operate upon entirely different presuppositions. The Christian believes the Bible; he believes that the Father must be obeyed. The unbeliever doesn't consider what God's demands are; to him, God is not his Father to be loved and obeyed.

I think that we are perhaps most vulnerable when we love. It is then our hearts risk being broken, but especially so when we Christians give our love and devotion to one with whom God has forbidden such intimacy. Love means caring whether we offend the loved one; it means oftentimes sacrificing our wishes. But when we care and sacrifice in a way which compromises our Christian principles, then we run into grave difficulty. Sinful compromise may be a way of life that erodes, though ever so gradually, our faith. Then both partners are in serious trouble, not to mention the children who are daily witnesses to the whole scene.

Marriage is not a tame horse easy to drive even for two totally committed Christians; it is a horse hard to manage when one Christian is committed and the other is not. But marriage is a horse impossible to manage well when one is Christian and the other not. If God holds the reins of both husband and wife—guiding, restraining, reassuring, controlling—we'll weather the ride because we ride with Christ in the driver's seat. He promises us that.

I am not implying that the marriage of two believers ensures constant, rapturous bliss—not without daily work, communion with each other in truth, and contact with God. But God is with us, if we keep the channel of prayer and trust open and if we seek earnestly His will in His Word. If we need help with problems to which we seem to find no answers, regardless of how hard we try to find them on our own, we can call upon fine Christian pastors or other Christian counselors for help to solve our problems in a scriptural way. We are not alone. Other Christians are with us, and God is for us because our homes are dear to Him—dear to Him because our families are part of the bride of Christ, and our homes are little centers of worship and training for young and old members of His Church. We must think upon how much God has loved us to give to two people the privilege of establishing a unit of such importance with such far-reaching consequences for the health of the Church.

There is nothing in this world more foundational to the Church, to society, to the very existence of humanity, than your home. Remember that a home was established in the very beginning by God—the home of Adam and Eve. Concerning the home, we must receive our directives from God's revealed Word. You will receive no support from society for God's commands concerning marriage "only in the Lord"; no support in training your children in the "nurture and admonition of the Lord"; no support for God's carefully defined roles for father as the head of his home—leader, prophet, priest and king—and mother as the faithful helper suitable for her husband.

"Experts" in today's society may tell you that children can be adequately trained to be whole persons by other social organizations or institutions outside of the home. Parents' roles are no longer important, they say; they can be switched around or eliminated. We are told that marriage is optional, even unnecessary, but God knows that the abolition of marriage and the Christian home would ruin society.

Others tell us that sexual problems are the chief source of rifts in marriage. I don't deny that great anguish can be caused by sexual maladjustment, but I agree with C. S. Lewis that this is not the root of the problem. He says, "It is marriage itself, not the marriage bed, that will be likely to hinder us from waiting uninterruptedly on God."[7] That is surely true. An unbeliever and believer might have what they consider to be a well-adjusted sex life, but the unremitting strain of belief against unbelief in a constant tug-of-war is what keeps the believing partner from a close, uninterrupted walk with His God; and this constant war of spirits has a devastating effect upon the life and attitudes of the unbelieving one as well. The sex life of both mates is affected, so the unifying effect that sex plays in the relationship is undermined.

Pictured in Ruth is the beautiful marriage of Ruth and Boaz. We can't read this account without experiencing real joy at seeing the happiness and stability of a marriage pleasing to God.

Boaz commends Ruth. She wanted to please God. Boaz wanted a virtuous wife; he was a godly man. A young Moabite widow converted to Israel's God, Ruth desired above all to have a marriage pleasing to God and to her faithful mother-in-law, Naomi. Ruth was not rich; she lived on alms.

---

[7]C. S. Lewis, *The Four Loves* (New York: Harcourt Brace Jovanovich, Inc., 1960), p. 137.

She is not said to be beautiful. It was her goodness, her inner spiritual beauty, most of all, that attracted Boaz. All of Ruth's neighbors agreed that she was a virtuous woman, the kind of woman mentioned in Proverbs 31 whose price is above rubies, who delights her husband—a woman a man can trust.

Ruth did not choose Boaz because he was young or handsome (the Bible says he was a wealthy elder), but she chose him to please God and her mother-in-law, Naomi. Ruth must have been attracted to Boaz because of his justness, tenderness, compassion, and faith. We are told Ruth did not seek younger men, rich or poor, but was willing to marry as the law and God intended her to, even though Boaz was an older man.

Boaz had prayed that God would reward Ruth for her courage and constancy; Boaz himself was the answer to his own prayer for Ruth in that he became her husband, lover, and protector. Through his prayers, Ruth received the kindness and love of God and was elevated from poverty to riches by God's grace, though she had not sought wealth.

Obed, the son born of this marriage, was an ancestor of Jesus Christ. Naomi, Obed's grandmother, had, under God, been the match-maker of this marriage. How marvelously God worked to keep His covenant through the families involved in this marriage. Obed's paternal grandmother had been a harlot, Rahab who hid Joshua's spies and later came to love God truly. Ruth had been a heathen Moabite. After these women came to know God, they made good wives for God's men.

Maybe you think your marriage could never mean so much in God's plan as Ruth's and Boaz's marriage. You might think, "Oh, well, God intended to bring about the coming of His own Son through *them*. *My* marriage has in it no promise of such miracles. But, stop, think a moment! Remember your standing with God in Jesus Christ: (1) you are His precious seed—His own dear child loved with the love the Father has for His only begotten son; (2) if you marry and have children, all of God's promises to be a God to you and your children are still in force just as they were for Ruth and Boaz; and (3) your home is the very foundation of the Christian Church. Don't you see the amazing, overwhelming privilege God has given to you? You are a progenitor of some of the members of the bride of Christ, by the power of the Holy Spirit. Christ's love rests upon you and your children. Nothing is more important than that. It is a miracle of grace.

So, Christian marriage has tremendous potential. We simply cannot imagine what our roles or the roles of our children will be in the plan and providence of God. We do know that our roles as restored images of God and our membership in the very body of Christ can never be without profound, eternal significance to God, to the Church, and to society.

6
YOUR MARRIAGE STRENGTHENS OR WEAKENS YOUR CHILDREN

Covenant children[1] are God's gift to us—olive plants around your table, He calls them (Ps. 128). Our homes are the greenhouses where the children grow, breathing the air of God's truth, putting down roots deep and strong in the fertile medium of God's Word and love. A half-way marriage makes a half-way home. Children will not grow strong in the Lord if the medium in which they grow is unbalanced, truth mixed with untruth.

In his growth a child has many needs, but his biggest need is in his soul, for his soul is born dead, stillborn; that is, his soul is unable to make a move toward God, the source of spiritual life and salvation, until it is regenerated (born again) by God the Holy Spirit. In its natural unregenerated (dead) state a soul keeps moving away from God. Parents must be committed to feeding the child the truth of God's Word, modeling the love of Christ to the child in trust that God's truth will be used to regenerate the child's heart. A child is blessed more than he can ever know if he has been placed by God in a totally Christian home with both parents devoted to the nurture of his soul in Jesus Christ. This care, this deep concern for his soul is the deepest love a parent can show him.

God knew that little ones need *two* Christian parents to love and train them in God's love and discipline. (Discipline is an important part of love.) This is one important reason, though not the *only* reason, He entreats us and commands us: marry *only* in the Lord.

Joshua said that union to an unbeliever is a threat to your soul. If it is a threat to the believer's soul, then it stands to reason it is a threat to your children's souls. A child needs security in this area of his soul's welfare as well as security in other areas of his life. In fact, if his soul is insecure, he suffers insecurity about his identity and his relationships with others. The solid secure foundation of a home built on Christ, both parents agreeing in their love and obedience to the Lord, is a necessity for the child's physical, emotional and spiritual security and maturity.

We who hold to Reformed doctrine[2] believe that our children are covenant children; that God in Scripture has covenanted to be our God and the

---

[1] The children of believers.

[2] As we mentioned before, "doctrine" means "teaching" and is not to be confused with dogma; of course we can be dogmatic about our teaching, but then so was Jesus.

God of our sons and daughters. By virtue of this eternal covenant our children are placed in a special position under God and Christian parents to receive, by God's grace and power alone, salvation in Christ.

Parents have the responsibility to train covenant children in the "nurture and admonition of the Lord," beseeching God for His grace in their hearts. Children are held responsible to accept the conditions of the covenant and to respond to God's grace by taking Christ as their own Lord and Saviour.

Perhaps some Christian reading this is married to an unbeliever, and you both want children. You should carefully examine your motives for having children. (All of us should.) The unbeliever (or believer) may want children to satisfy his own emotional needs. You may hope that children will break down the barriers between you and your unbelieving mate. But, really, children may further alienate you from each other, especially so if you seriously desire to train them to become conformed to the image of Christ. Little Christ-like images usually displease an unbelieving parent. Indeed, genuine animosity can be, and often is, generated by such a situation.

The Christian home doesn't exist for its own sake, nor for the sake of the marriage itself, nor for children alone. It exists to glorify our wonderful, sovereign, triune God. In the home the Lamb of God is Head, with the earthly parent, the husband and father, in authority under God. The husband and wife are to cultivate a oneness with each other in Christ which continues after the children leave home, a oneness patterned after the union of Christ and His bride, the Church.

The Christian home is the training ground for the little members of Christ's body. Every covenant child who arrives at personal faith in Christ's atoning death for his sins and who loves Jesus Christ as Lord and Saviour strengthens the bride of Christ. This truth is implicit in all of Scripture. It is in the home, the basic and most important institution of society, that little Christians are to be loved with the love of Christ, and exhorted, counseled, and educated in the Lord by their parents; they are to be shaped by the Holy Spirit to become conformed to the image of Christ. There is no better place given by God than the Christian home for such training; *father* and *mother* in fellowship with God the Son, Jesus Christ—the "Holy Triangle."[3] The Christian school and the Church are to supplement the training in the Christian home, but they may never supplant it.

Parents are God's models for their children. I think in particular of one

---

[3] Joel Nederhood, *The Holy Triangle* (Grand Rapids: Baker Book House, 1946); I heartily recommend this fine book.

of my grandsons, a four-year-old whose father is of Scottish Reformed heritage. I see that little boy smile his father's winsome smile. I hear him speak with his father's accent as he repeats his father's words. I see him bow his curly head and clasp his little hands as we say grace. In so many ways he is a tiny replica of his dad.

Whether his father is always thinking of it or not, he is his little son's model—day in, day out. So, if he intends to inculcate a biblical way of living into our grandson's life, he must practice a completely biblical life-style himself. If he doesn't, then little Stephen will form bad habits for living and for handling his sinful nature, because children are great imitators.

Children are our disciples as we instruct them in Christian living in the home. An unbelieving parent cannot help children acquire the goal God has set for every Christian, whether covenant child or adults. That goal or purpose of God for life is that the Christian become like Jesus, conformed to His image. Both father and mother must have the same desire to help their child along the road to this goal. Unbelieving fathers or mothers have no desire whatever to do this. They travel a different road. Indeed, they have other goals for their children, many of which are diametrically opposed to the aims of a believing mate. Unbelievers, instead of habituating their children in Christian practices, will habituate them in patterns opposed to God's patterns and plans. That is inevitable and tragic.

God has made it very clear that parents are to discipline their children in habits of godliness, helping them to achieve the skills for Christian living. This takes years of hourly, daily effort and cooperation on the part of both parents.[4] Patience and perseverance given only by God are needed to direct and train a child in righteousness. An unbelieving partner lacks the desire and ability to train a child in the Lord. This leaves the believing parent with the whole responsibility of properly structuring the thinking and life-style of the child toward his Saviour. The believer himself is left without the spiritual support of the husband or wife. No one is there to help him or her become more like Christ.

The child should see *both* of his parents becoming more conformed to Christ's image and more unified in spirit and soul. The child needs both parents as models acting more and more like Christ in their relationship to each other, to the children, and to others.

The daily contemplation of God's Word together, the daily communion

---

[4] Deuteronomy 7:6.

of souls united with the Saviour, closely bind two Christians and their children together in His love. Faith is strengthened; zest for living and joy even in trying circumstances increase as God guides and comforts. Peace and harmony and union are the fruits of hearts forgiven and washed in the blood of Jesus' redemptive sacrifice. Doubt and mistrust are taken away, not multiplied.

Only in marriage is such a uniquely profound intimacy imposed upon two people. The spiritual condition of one partner deeply affects and influences the other for good or evil. No wonder Jesus asked if two are able to walk together except they be agreed, let alone *live* and *sleep* together. When two are not agreed, an explosive situation of highly charged negative and positive beliefs, motives, and attitudes arises. Children are quick to notice. Their trust in their parents is damaged. And because a child's parents are in authority under God, and represent God to the child, his faith in God is damaged, too.

A tragic account of a son, the victim of such an environment, is given in Leviticus 24:10-16. His mother was Israelitish; his father, Egyptian. It is very probable that the tension in that home was great if the father was in disagreement with the mother. Anyway, the son, who wandered outside the camp of Israel, got into a struggle with a man of Israel. He swore and cursed and blasphemed the holy name of the Lord. In all of this he may have been copying the model his father had set for him. He paid for his blasphemy with his own life (and perhaps his soul), and the mother, Shelomith of the tribe of Dan, lost her son.

One commentator remarks that this incident may be recorded "to point out the ungodly issue of so unholy an alliance, and to guard the Hebrew women against intermarriage with heathen." Matthew Henry, remarking upon this story, says that children are apt to take after the worst side, whichever it is, and will "sooner learn of an Egyptian father to blaspheme, than of an Israelitish mother to pray and praise."

If the husband and father is an unbeliever, there is really no head of the home in the proper Christian sense. "A home without a head is an invitation to chaos. It spells derangement and disaster worse even than that which results when a nation is without a ruler. . . ."[5] The perfectly structured Christian home must follow God's perfect plan: father as head, mother as suitable helper, and children as their disciples. I say this is His

---

[5] William Hendriksen, *New Testament Commentary on Ephesians* (Grand Rapids: Baker Book House, 1967), p. 248.

perfect arrangement for a Christian home. I am not saying that Christian homes with *two* believing parents can ever be *perfect*. No. We must honestly admit that two Christian parents may fail in many things: in showing compassion, in honesty, in true communication—many things. We are only sinners saved by grace. God has work to do on us until the day we will be perfect, when we reach heaven. But perfection is our goal: to try (as perfectly as we can) to reflect Christ's image. We must be truthful, admit our sins, and start again. Christians desire this. Sinners don't. That is what I am saying.

Little children are "greenhouse" plants. We can't safely subject them to the cold, wintry blasts of unbelief. The climate supplied by a "bad match" cannot supply the proper warmth for them. They are tender plants, the spiritual seed of Abraham, tender young shoots of the Vine, Jesus Christ. He cherished them with deepest love and concern. That is one big reason He insists upon *two* Christian parents to minister to their spiritual growth.[6]

Only Christian parents can nurture little Christians. Yet how often many true believers expect an unbelieving mate to be a good father or mother to Christ's own little ones. Unbelievers cannot, will not, keep God's covenant to train children in the Lord because by nature they are covenant breakers.

Here where I live in the country by a river, I have opportunity to observe in nature a great variety of adult animals and birds caring for their young. I have never seen—nor expect to see—the rabbits care for baby birds. Their whole way of life differs. Rabbits are grounded. Birds fly. Rabbits are vegetarians. Birds eat worms and insects. The only possible way a rabbit could raise a baby bird would be for God to supernaturally change that rabbit into a different creature, a bird. Then the rabbit could perform all the tasks necessary to house and feed a bird, and could properly communicate with the bird, could show and tell the bird how to live the role of "birdness."

That being true in the animal kingdom, it is astounding how many times we see a Christian who thinks that an unbelieving mate can help him or her to raise baby Christians to Christlikeness. Well, he can't. Like the rabbit, he needs to be transformed into a new, a different creature to take care of covenant children. We can't expect a parent who is still at enmity with God, who spurns the precious blood of Jesus Christ, to be the least bit concerned with training them to know God, the least bit concerned whether the

---

[6]Elisabeth Elliot has some good guidelines for choosing a Christian husband so that two married *Christians* can be compatible: *Let Me Be a Woman* (Wheaton: Tyndale House Publishers, 1976), pp. 68-71.

children ever reach their God-ordained destiny to be conformed to the image of Christ. How can unbelievers care? They don't know Jesus themselves.

Then how do we believers ever arrive at the place that we think it matters little to God whom we marry?

We have talked about the effect of an unbelieving father or mother upon covenant children. Let's now consider another influence not generally supposed to be so important to the child's welfare: in-laws.

So many times we hear young people about to marry say, "Well, this is our private affair. After all, I'm not marrying the whole family!" That is only partly true. You do marry only one person, but that one person didn't come into being spontaneously without any forbears. Unless his whole family has died,he brings into your circle several others besides himself, persons with whom you must communicate, fraternize, play, eat, and fellowship—unless you move too far away for these things. (Even then, you'll no doubt get letters or calls which won't edify or which may not contribute to the tranquility of your home.)

Unbelieving in-laws may influence you and your mate—and particularly your children—in an evil way. In II Chronicles 19:2 Jehu reproves Jehoshaphat for fraternizing with Ahab. Jehoshaphat took Athaliah as a wife for his son. She was the daughter of wicked Ahab. Now Jehoshaphat was a good king of Judah. He worshiped Jehovah, not the gods of Baalim, although the people of Judah were still sacrificing on the high places. The Lord prospered him. Jehoshaphat removed the high places of idol worship; he put the remaining Sodomites out of the land. But he joined King Ahab, Athaliah's father, in war against the Syrians. That's when Jehu reproved him for joining Ahab.

Jehoshaphat's choice of a wicked wife for his son, Jehoram, had a devastating influence. It is mentioned three times that Jehoram was the son-in-law of Ahab, no doubt to stress Ahab's evil influence on Jehoram to do wickedness against his God. Jehoram had once done the deeds of his father, King Jehoshaphat, who had doubtless trained his son in the good knowledge of the Lord. How sad it is to see a good man's son finally dying "of sore diseases . . . without being desired" and no person regretting his death.

Athaliah was no spiritual help at all to Jehoram, nor to her son, Ahaziah, who succeeded his father to the throne of Judah. Athaliah's impious mother, Jezebel, had taught her well. In II Chronicles 22:3-4 we read that Ahaziah "walked in the ways of the house of Ahab, for his mother [Athaliah] was his counselor to do wickedly. And he did evil in the sight of the Lord like the house of Ahab, for they were his counselors after the death of his father, to his destruction." His mother's relatives caused his ruin. After he was dead, Athaliah "rose and destroyed all the royal offspring of the house of Judah" (v. 10), her own grandchildren! Only Joash was saved because his aunt, Ahaziah's sister, hid him from Athaliah.

Now today we don't seem to think much about how unbelieving in-laws can devastate our children, but we should not underestimate the tragic moral and spiritual effect they may have. It especially grieves God when we weaken little ones by bad influences we have carelessly chosen. It is wonderfully supportive to know that your marriage ties you not only with another believer but with believing in-laws who will strive to make your marriage meaningful, well-knit, and Christian—persons who will contribute to making the body of Christ stronger because they make you and your family stronger. God cares deeply about this good effect upon His Church. His blessing is on any effort to build up the bride, and His disfavor is upon all those who would cause a Christian to sin and weaken His bride.

Isaac had this strengthening of Israel in mind when he sent Jacob to Paddam-aram, to the house of his father-in-law, Laban—Rachel's father. He told Jacob, "You shall not take a wife from the daughters of Canaan." Isaac wanted Jacob to have a believing wife. He knew that was the only way to have God's blessing and to keep God's covenant as an heir of the promise of God to make them a special people. Jacob must not be "unequally yoked with an unbeliever" (II Cor. 6:16); he may not take a pagan wife, and neither may we.

Abraham's nephew, Lot, was not edified by his unbelieving sons-in-law. They did not see eye to eye with him in the things of the Lord. When Lot warned them of the impending destruction of Sodom, he appeared to his sons-in-law to be jesting. God's Word was foolishness to them. They ignored Lot. They were no different from unbelieving sons-in-law today who slight all concern for their souls or who make light of the things of God. We can't expect such men to care for the spiritual needs of their wives and children, nor for the Church.

Moses had a father-in-law who was a blessing to him. Jethro was a Midianite; the Midianites were descendants of Abraham by Keturah. They did acknowledge the true God, but it is not thought likely that they knew God among themselves as "Jehovah." Jethro, though a Midianite, was admitted into fellowship with Moses and Aaron. He offered sacrifices to the true God and partook of the sacrificial meal with Moses and Aaron.

When Jethro saw how much Moses was doing for the people of Israel, judging and counseling, he told Moses that he was going to wear himself out. "The task is too heavy for you," he said. "The thing you are doing is not good. Now listen to me and I will give you counsel, and God be with you." Then he told Moses how to delegate authority among the people to assist him.

Now many sons-in-law would not have taken so kindly to the advice of Jethro, but Moses "listened to his father-in-law, and did all that he had said." After farewells, Jethro "went his way into his own land." He did not stay to check up on Moses. And I imagine Moses appreciated that.

Though a priest of Midian, it is not likely that Jethro's knowledge of the true God was as full as Moses' knowledge since Moses had received direct revelation from God. And probably Zipporah, Jethro's daughter and Moses' wife, though a believer in the true God, shared her father's lack of knowledge. This was evidenced in her repugnance toward the rite of circumcision for Eliezer their son. Perhaps we could say that Zipporah was of a different "denomination" than was Moses: one, an Israelite; the other, a Midianite with faulty knowledge, which can cause problems even between two persons who are true believers. This seemingly small difference of belief caused great grief of mind and heart. Moses got sick. Zipporah was frightened and maybe angry and rebellious. But though Zipporah and Moses did not agree about God's ordinance of circumcision, God did bless them because they had a basic mutual faith and love for Him. Their sons became Levites, those highly favored of the Lord to carry out the priestly duties in the tabernacle. Even though God richly blessed them, I think we can safely assume that Moses and Zipporah would have been much happier if they had agreed on all points of doctrine. So-called little disagreements can be extremely erosive of harmony.

In the accounts above of the influence of in-laws, we read no comments from the children involved. But that is not because God is not concerned with the children. Jesus spoke of the judgment upon those who cause His children to stumble.

The children of mixed marriages were a chief concern of Nehemiah (Neh. 13), along with the profaning of the temple by a priest, Eliashib, who had married a heathen Ammonite, and the profaning of the Sabbath day by the selling and buying of all kinds of wares in the city on the Sabbath. These three states of affair indicated spiritual degeneration of God's people. In his efforts to reform things, Nehemiah remarks that he saw that the Jews had married women from Ashdod, Ammon, and Moab. He was especially grieved when he heard their children speaking in the language of these people and none of the children able to speak the language of Judah. Nehemiah was so righteously angry with the Israelites that he contended with them, making them swear by God, "You shall not give your daughters to their sons, nor take of their daughters for your sons or for yourselves." Nehemiah prayed fervently for them and then for himself.

I am sure that the fact the children could speak another language was not what distressed Nehemiah; no doubt it was because their words were impious, impure, or corrupt—certainly not what we expect from the mouths of "babes and sucklings." The unbelieving mothers were stumbling blocks to their children. Jesus would have agreed with Nehemiah in his concern for them, for He said it is better to have a millstone tied about one's neck and be thrown into the deepest sea than to do harm to the souls of the littlest members of His body.

Sometimes I think we don't stop to consider that the tiniest parts of Christ's body are most important to Him. We cannot say that because they are so small and naive they are insignificant. Surely we must take stock of the future damage we will be causing them when we assent to mixed marriages; we must think ahead, realizing that when we weaken the children of the Church by a bad marriage, we weaken the entire body of believers.

If we don't think about this seriously, we will find ourselves contributing to the harm of the Church. Our covenant children are the godly line of the Lord. Francis Schaeffer says, " . . . there is constant prohibition throughout the Old and New Testament against the people of God marrying those who are not of the people of God. The Old Testament says repeatedly: If you marry those who are not God's people, and if you give your sons and daughters to them, *the godly line will be destroyed*."[7]

Doesn't this dreadful, spine-chilling prediction grip *your* heart in an agony of responsibility to God and to future generations? Perhaps in no sadder way do we see the actual fulfillment of the visiting of the iniquities of the fathers unto the third and fourth generations mentioned in the Ten Commandments. Judges 2:10-17 records that there arose another generation who didn't know the Lord. They had no knowledge of all the wonder-

---

[7] Francis A. Schaeffer, *Genesis in Space and Time* (Inter-Vasity Press, 1972), p. 126.

ful things God had done for Israel. They abandoned the Lord and served Baal.

The destruction of the godly line is a tragedy striking to the very heart of the Bridegroom because the godly line is the bride of Christ. May we never hurt the bride, nor her Bridegroom, by our own disobedience to God's command, "Marry only in the Lord."

7
YOUR MARRIAGE STRENGTHENS OR WEAKENS THE CHURCH

Let's take a look at some of the treacherous marriages of believers to unbelievers recorded for us in the Old Testament. We can learn much from them.

After their fall into sin, Adam and Eve had two sons. Cain was the wicked one, Abel, the righteous one. Cain murdered Abel in a fit of rage and resentment. Then God banished Cain from His presence. Adam and Eve were deprived of both of their sons. We can only imagine their grief after that sad event. But God gave them another son, Seth, the godly seed He had promised to them. It was then that men began to call upon the name of the Lord. But not Cain. He did not worship God. His descendants lived in tents and tended sheep. They also made musical instruments, the harp and organ, and Tubal-cain was a famous worker in brass and iron.

Seth was destined to perpetuate the Church; from him the Messiah, Jesus Christ, would come.

In Genesis 6 is the first mention of God's chosen people marrying unbelievers. Men were multiplying on the earth and daugthers were born to them. The sons of God[1] saw the daughters of these men who didn't know God. They noticed that the girls were very fair and beautiful. Can't you hear the wows of admiration and sense the quickened heartbeat as the siren allure of these forbidden beauties called to the passion of men of God who seemed to rush headlong into marriage with them? Quite likely their precipitous leap into union with these women was occasioned by a loss of love for God and His standards which began long before they saw the beautiful daughters of mėn. Defection from God is not usually as instantaneous as it sometimes appears to be. For instance, David saw Bathsheba and desired her for his wife, but I think probably he had admired her for some time, looking at her from afar every day, perhaps, until he could no longer resist plotting how to obtain her for his own.

It seems that beauty of face and form were as important to these men of long ago as television and magazine advertisements tell us it is today. Beauty has always been a prime consideration. I think of a handsome young fellow who once complained to me that he couldn't find a girl. Just

[1] See *Exposition of Genesis*, H. C. Leupold (pp. 250, 253) for an explanation of the term "sons of God." Most expositors agree with this interpretation.

then a very plain but very charming, stylish girl walked by. "There goes one. She's a lovely girl," I said. He shrugged. "Beauty isn't everything," I offered. "No," he answered, "but it sure helps."

Well, those sons of God in Genesis 6 seemed to think physical beauty was *everything*. These sons were descendants of Seth, the godly son of Adam and Eve. The gorgeous women were of the Cainites, descendants of the wicked Cain who killed his own brother, Abel. Without delay the sons of God married these women for mere lust of beauty. They took wives for themselves, "whomever they chose," the Bible says. These sons of the triune God neglected to consider the religious beliefs of these girls; they placed face and form above piety and goodness. They took the girls *they* chose without advice from God.

Verse 4 indicates that the children of these marriages were mighty men, perhaps stalwart and handsome and brave; but they were violent and wicked, for verse 5 tells us that "the Lord saw that the wickedness of man was great on the earth." Worst of all, their depravity of heart was so gross that God said " . . . every intent of the thoughts of his heart was only evil continually." Wickedness and violence was *great* upon the earth. What a frightful outcome, mainly because children beloved of God failed to choose believing mates. They failed to keep their part of the covenant God had made with them to be their God and the God of their children. Instead they deliberately chose evil. No good could be found anywhere.

The most dreadful thing was that they caused their loving God great grief of heart. Believers are warned not to grieve the Holy Spirit. Only Noah and his family found favor in God's sight. These covenant-breaking marriages resulted in nothing but corruption and violence. The sons of God were ruined by their sinful choice of marriage partners, and not only they but their children and grandchildren suffered immeasurably—even the loss of their souls. Here they were, God's godly line of people, chosen by Him to be members of Christ's body—covenant people who did not cherish their position in the family of God. Can't you see why God was grieved?

There must have been many heartbroken parents, too, who wept for these marriages. I suppose there were tearful pleas and anguished prayers offered for these foolish young people.

Esau's marriage to two heathen women (he should have known better) caused great grief to his parents. In Genesis 26:34, 35 we read, "And when Esau was forty years old he married Judith the daughter of Beeri the Hittite, and Basemath the daughter of Elon the Hittite." Now Esau was a covenant child (an older one to be sure, but still a covenant child). He despised his covenant standing, so perhaps he felt that his marriages were private matters since, not being a believer himself, it mattered little whom he married.

But it did matter. Isaac and Rebekah, his parents, were deeply affected by his choice. (I'm glad Isaac is mentioned, too, or we might, as is usually done, place the blame for trouble upon mother-in-law, Rebekah.) In Genesis 27:46 Rebekah said to Isaac, "I am tired of living because of the daughters of Heth; if Jacob takes a wife from the daughters of the land, what good will my life be to me?"

Even though we may think Rebekah overreacted to the situation, family relations must have been strained to the breaking point for Rebekah to have made such a strong statement of despair. Communication must have been practically nonexistent, for what did Esau's unbelieving wives have in common with Rebekah? Certainly not the same spiritual beliefs and maybe not much else in common either. Rebekah's life was miserable, and Jacob, the other son, must have been adversely affected by his parents' misery. And think of the poor testimony of Esau's disobedience to their unbelieving friends and to other covenant children.

Such marriages as Esau's violated the great principle laid down by Abraham in Genesis 24:3-4 to his servant, the oldest of his household, ". . . I will make you swear by the Lord, the God of heaven and the God of earth, that you shall not take a wife for my son from the daughters of the Canaanites among whom I live, but you shall go to my country and to my relatives, and take a wife for my son Isaac."

Esau is even called a fornicator in Hebrews 12:16. No wonder Isaac and Rebekah regarded his conduct with "grief of mind," anger, sorrow, resentment and righteous indignation.

When Esau knew that his father forbade Jacob to marry a Canaanite,he went to Ishmael (another unbeliever) and married, besides the wives he had, Mahalath, the daughter of Ishmael, Abraham's son who had married an Egyptian.

Esau had a fatal weakness for choosing wrongly. It seems he tried to please his father, Isaac, only. We aren't told that he wanted to please God. So he compounded his sin, adding even more grief to grief for the people of God, for from his wife, Mahalath, arose the tribe of Kedar from which Mohammed ultimately came. As history has proved, followers of Mohammed became some of the most relentless foes of the Christian Church.

No doubt the thoughts of Isaac and Rebekah projected into the future, imagining some of the horrors which could result of such a union. They must have feared for their grandchildren and for the people of God. Of course, God could see without any speculation just what would surely be the outcome.

From these marriages of Esau came the Edomites who were enemies of the congregation (the Church) of Israel. The Herods, one of whom condemned Jesus to death, were Idumaeans, or Edomites. Again history shows Esau's choice of life partners was just his own personal business which concerned only him and his wives. The influence of his heathen children and their progeny was devastating to the Church of God, to his parents, and to their God. The descendants of Esau were the *enemies* of God's people right down to the time of Christ.

I think that we who say we love Christ, who have been washed in His precious blood, need to stop thinking like naturalistic unbelievers, particularly in choosing marriage partners. Francis Schaeffer calls this kind of thinking "unfaith." The Christian who claims supernatural salvation, and who should view everything from the supernatural perspective, many times is exercising *unfaith* as he looks at areas of his life or even his world from a naturalistic instead of supernatural point of view. He may look at choosing the person he marries in this way. This is a tragedy for him, his children, and the Church.

Perhaps you haven't thought much about the effect of marriages upon the Church. Though He wasn't speaking of mixed marriages specifically, in Deuteronomy 24:4 God said that other kinds of unscriptural marriages would bring sin upon the land of Israel. It is still true that ungodly marriages bring sin upon the Church.

As we noted earlier, Balaam,[2] the false prophet, knew this only too well. Urged by Balak, king of Moab, to curse Israel, Balaam protested and demonstrated that he was powerless to curse God's beloved people. But he knew a more effective strategy; his parting advice, we are told in Revelation 2:14, was for Balak to use a more cunning way to seduce Israel from their God: the charms of the beautiful women of Moab and Midian. Though Balaam's donkey showed more wisdom than his master, the evil craftiness of Balaam led the Israelites to idolatry. There was no need for bloodshed, violence, or anything that would cause Israel to suspect their spiritual peril. The way to ruin was paved with good food, beautiful women, and wicked

---

[2]Numbers 31:16

titillation of mind and spirit in pleasurable though forbidden friendship with strange gods.

So when the men of Israel were invited to the sacrifices of these false gods, they ate; and then they bowed down to the gods. "Israel joined himself to Baal-peor." Notice again that the Bible wastes no words: they were invited, they ate, they bowed, then they *joined.* Immediately these people of God were enticed away from union with Him, into spiritual adultery. They were conquered not by the armies of Moab, but by lust for beautiful women and their false gods. Though they were almost in the land of Canaan where they could feast on God's favor, they threw it all away because they did not treasure their covenant relationship to God who loved them so much.

If we are not careful we too can easily despise God's marvelous, gracious covenant. It is this same despising of God's covenant that causes the Church such shame and grief when a Christian marries an unbeliever. Really, in the final analysis, it indicates a lack of proper love for God. (We all lack love for Him to some degree, of course, because as long as we are on this earth we will not love Him fully.)

Israel's decline was nothing less than whoredom in God's sight, and His righteous anger was turned against the adulterous nation. A plague broke out and many people died. Doesn't "plague" of some sort—physical, emotional, or spiritual—always follow defection from God? In the case of Israel both kinds of adultery had been committed—spiritual and physical. I believe Francis Schaeffer has said (I can't remember where) that often physical adultery follows spiritual adultery. When we place our love for God second to an idol, it follows that we also place other desires above keeping his law. Our absolutes are no longer black and white. They are colored shades of gray by rationalizing our own sinful wishes and desires.

Our bad choices are so tragic, not only for the sorrow they bring, but because they show how cold our love for God has grown. In the war we wage between good and evil, we Christians constantly battle—the old man against the new man, our own evil desires against God's good and perfect will. Satan with diabolical cunning exploits our weaknesses. He never tires of making ridiculous imitations of God's most beautiful gifts and institutions. Poor marriages, unchristian marriages, delight him. With indefatigable, malicious joy he labors to divert our beautiful, God-given feelings and sexual desires to ignoble or base purposes. He knows that once he can turn our desire to those who do not love Christ, or to other idols, we will then begin to rationalize, defend our bad choices and bad consciences, and sin against God by forgetting our covenant obligations to Him. This is what happened to Israel. God graciously makes them an example to us.

In Ezekiel 18:29-31 God told Israel that if they repented they would not die because of their spiritual whoredom. He was merciful. He says:

> But the house of Israel says, "The way of the Lord is not right." Are my ways not right, O house of Israel? Is it not your ways that are not right? Therefore I will judge you, O house of Israel, each according to his conduct . . . . Repent and turn away from all your transgressions, so that iniquity may not become a stumbling block to you. Cast away from you your transgressions which you have committed, and make yourselves a new heart and a new spirit! For why will you die, O house of Israel?

Today God speaks to you and to me as members of spiritual Israel. He warns us of spiritual adultery. He says we are betrothed to Him, married to Him (Hos. 2:19). To know God in this intimate way through Jesus Christ our Bridegroom is the most important thing in all the world. Any person or thing that captures our affection or captivates our hearts—husbands, wives, children, fame, money—anything which takes first place in our hearts above God causes us to commit spiritual adultery. Our love must first of all be for God our beloved Bridegroom. "And I will say to those who were not My people, 'You are My people!' And they will say, 'Thou art my God!'" We are His; He is ours. We must not deal treacherously with Him to whom we belong.

You would think that Solomon, the wisest man who ever lived, would have realized that God hated mixed marriages. He was surely familiar with the teachings in Proverbs 31 in which the mother of King Lemuel (who, it is thought, could have been Solomon himself) warned him that strange women could destroy kings.[3] His own father's (David) defection from God because of strange women should have been a warning to Solomon. After he was king, Solomon formed a marriage alliance with Pharaoh's daughter. The marriage was probably a political expediency favored in those times, a wrong motive for marriage. Solomon brought his new wife to the city of David ". . . until he had finished building his own house and the house of the Lord and the wall around Jerusalem." At that time, we are told, Solomon did love the Lord and was keeping the statutes of his father, David.

---

[3]You Christian fellows are kings under Christ; yet an unbelieving wife can destroy your fellowship with God. Marry only princesses or queens of God's royal household.

It may be that this particular wife of Solomon was a true convert. And it may be that she and Solomon had some trying differences regarding spiritual matters; it is very likely they did. There seems to be nothing said about God's displeasure with the marriage. But we do know that I Kings 11:1 tells us that Solomon loved many foreign, or heathen, women later on, and that *they* turned his heart away after other gods. God had promised him great things, but Solomon forfeited these things by intermarriage with unbelievers. Verse 6 says *he did evil*. Solomon had directly defied God's command, "You shall not associate with them, neither shall they associate with you, for they will surely turn your heart away after their gods." And that is exactly what happened: "Solomon held fast to these [unbelievers] in love . . . . his wives turned his heart away . . . . away after other gods; and his heart was not wholly devoted to the Lord His God, as the heart of David his father had been" (vv. 2-4).

Solomon went after the things his wives loved; after Ashtoreth, the goddess of the Sidonians, and after Milcom, the detestable idol. It seems to us unthinkable that so wise a man as Solomon, because he wished to please his wicked wives, could set up altars to Moloch, the very god to whom his forbears had sacrificed their children. No wonder his kingdom became divided!

In Psalm 106:34-38 David, recounting the rebellion and deliverance of Israel, says they were rebellious against the Spirit of God: "They did not destroy the peoples [the heathen captives] as the Lord commanded them but they mingled with the nations, and learned their practices, and served their idols, which became a snare to them. They even sacrificed their sons and their daughters to the demons, and shed innocent blood . . . ." David said they played spiritual harlotry because of their close associations with unbelievers.

Ezra suffered deep grief caused by the sin of intermarriage of believers with unbelievers. "You have been unfaithful and have married foreign wives adding to the guilt of Israel." As leader of his flock, Ezra did not minimize their awful betayal of their covenant relationship to God. It was no private matter! He was especially concerned because their betrayal had brought guilt to the body of believers. This is precisely what we do to the Church of God when we wilfully contract marriage with an unbeliever. Such marriages cause insurmountable problems for the believer and the unbelieving partner, for parents, pastors, elders, and other church members. But worst of all, the harm is done to God's beloved bride as a unit, a wrong He will never tolerate. The men of Israel trembled because of the seriousness of this sin.

Judges 3 relates that Israel married Canaanites in defiance of God's command to them. Then they forsook their God. Do you see the connection between marriage to an unbeliever and turning from God to other idols which take His place? Here and elsewhere in Scripture this turning from God to idols is represented under the similitude of whoredom. Why? Because it is the violation of a marriage covenant with God, forsaking Him and taking a strange god to love, to intimately embrace. Israel served idols with the good things God had given them: His oil, His incense, His food and their own children whom He called "My children." These children were the future Church. They were God's own possession, born into God's own house. They bore the sign and seal[4] of the covenant but had been sacrificed to devils instead of dedicated to Him.

Israel was unfaithful to God even though He had promised them: "I will never break my covenant with you." God is a faithful spouse. Because Israel had allowed the Canaanites to remain in the land and had intermarried among them, God said He would not drive the Canaanites out for them; they would become thorns to them and whips on their sides, He said—a constant, painful nettling to them. This fact should cause any Christian to greatly fear breaking the marriage laws of our covenant God, for we then forfeit His help which we so desperately need to have a successful marriage.

The parents of Israel sinned in all of this, too. They forgot God. From these heathen Canaanites they took daughters for their sons and gave their daughters to Canaanite men to marry. The parents themselves even married some of them. And they served their Gods: Baalim and the groves. In unequal matches the bad usually overcomes the good, just as when a good apple is affected by the closeness of the bad apple in the barrel. (This tired but true adage still applies.)

Israel, by willfully succumbing to a false god, forgot the true God—out of sight, out of mind. They forgot their union with Him, the uniqueness of His special love and favor and His betrothal to them. They did "what was right in their own eyes." When they came under bitter bondage to the king of Mesopotamia, they then cried to the Lord. And do you know that in mercy He raised up a deliverer for them (Judges 3:8, 9)? Though they didn't

[4]Circumcision in the Old Testament and baptism in the New Testament.

deserve it, He did not reject their pleas to Him. When we sincerely repent, He restores our hope and forgive us.

It was in his farewell address to God's people that Joshua gave warning to them. Joshua was 110 years old. Israel was at rest, but Joshua was keenly aware that the careless choice of unbelieving marriage partners could be their downfall again. It is significant that one of the last things he urges upon them is to be faithful to God by not marrying His enemies:

> Be very firm . . . . cling to the Lord your God . . . . take diligent heed to yourselves to love the Lord your God. For if you ever go back and cling to the rest of these nations, these which remain among you, and intermarry with them, so that you associate with them and they with you, know with certainty that the Lord your God will not continue to drive these nations out from before you; but they shall be a snare and a trap to you, and a whip in your sides and thorns in your eyes, until you perish from off this good land . . . . When you transgress the covenant of the Lord your God, which He commanded you, and go and serve other gods, and bow down to them, then the anger of the Lord will burn against you . . . (Josh. 23:6-16).

Joshua told Israel that the Church, the nation, would be ruined. And it was their own responsibility. Just as good comes from obeying God, evil comes from disobeying Him. His law holds eternally.

The terror of the Lord for our disobedience to his law is nothing to play around with. By disobedience to Him we bring unhappiness and destruction upon our own heads. God is not to blame. We are. We are like Israel so many times. We are not as wise as the ox and the ass mentioned in the Bible who "know their master's crib" and obey him.

Often at sunset on summer evenings, my husband and I watch the great blue heron descend with a giant flapping of his great wings on the opposite shore of our narrow river. Like a prince he regally measures his steps. Cautiously he watches for any enemy as he feeds along the shallows. At our slightest move he is up and away. He does not tarry for just one more fish, though they jump in sparkling profusion, tempting him to stay and indulge himself. This majestic creature, though made lower than man, shows more regard for his safety than often we do. We do not flee evil in this matter of marrying unbelievers, but we actively and deliberately pursue it.

> Ephraim mixes himself with the nations;
> Ephraim has become a cake not turned.
> Strangers devour his strength,

Yet he does not know it . . . .
So Ephraim has become like a silly dove, without sense . . . .
Woe to them, for they have strayed from Me!
Destruction is theirs, for they have rebelled against Me.
I would redeem them, but they speak lies against Me.
And they do not cry to Me from their heart . . .
They turn away from Me . . . .
Although I trained and strengthened their arms,
Yet they devise evil against Me.

Ephraim is called "a cake not turned." *Not turned*—only half-baked. This describes Israel once she prostituted her relationship with God by mixing with unbelievers in intimate union. Think of a pancake, brown on one side, pale and uncooked on the other. That was Ephraim—unattractive and repulsive to God, half-baked and incomplete once she betrayed her trust in God. The mismatched ingredients of different religions in this unappetizing "cake" would not blend in harmony as they should blend in a good recipe. God said, "O, Ephraim, you have played the harlot." It seemed He was always reminding them of that. Israel has defiled itself. Their deeds will not allow them to return to their God. Their sins mar their communion with God. For a spirit of harlotry is within them, and they do not know the Lord.

And that is the way it is with us the covenant people of God, when we marry someone who does not know our God. Like Israel, we have "dealt treacherously against the Lord" who bought us with His own precious blood. God cannot regard such an act lightly; He is angry with us and has every right to be angry. We in our foolishness reap the whirlwind when, like Israel, we do not distinguish ourselves from the heathen as God distinguishes us. We are clearly labeled His by Him. Hosea goes on to say (8:7, 8), "For they sow the wind, and they reap the whirlwind. Israel is swallowed up; they are now among the nations like a vessel in which no one delights." Israel's land was eaten up. They were impoverished by the very strangers in whom they had delighted. Their former loves held them in contempt. They lost their credibility and reputation. They were spiritually bankrupt.

In Malachi 2:11 we have the last Old Testament mention by God of the sin of intermarriage: "Judah has dealt treacherously, and an abomination has been committed in Israel and in Jerusalem; for Judah has profaned the sanctuary of the Lord which He loves, and has married the daughter of a foreign god." Notice that God's objection had nothing whatever to do with the race or nation of the wives; the harm was in the fact that the strangers

Israel married worshipped idols—they are called daughters of a "foreign" god. Israel was called by God, "holiness unto the Lord." They were dedicated to the true God as distinguished from their neighbors. They had showed contempt for the incredible identity with Himself that God had given only to them.

God then tells them of another offense: "And there is another thing you do: you cover the altar of the Lord with tears, with weeping and groaning, because He no longer regards the offering or accepts it with favor from your hand. Yet you say, 'For what reason?' Because the Lord has been a witness between you and the wife of your youth, against whom you have dealt treacherously, though she is the companion and your wife by covenant. But not one has done so who has a remnant of the Spirit . . ." (Mal. 2:13-15a).

In verse 17 God told Israel, "You have wearied the Lord with your words. Yet you say, 'How have we wearied Him?' In that you say, 'Everyone who does evil is good in the sight of the Lord, and He delights in them,' or, 'Where is the God of justice?' " God was weary with hearing them justify their bad marriages and divorces and faulty worship. They seemed to think God delighted in them despite their awful defection from His covenant.

Surely this is a tragic picture of what can happen today or in any age if we take lightly our covenant standing with God. We are priests and children of God. He is to be reverenced and obeyed as our loving Father and Master. In Malachi 1:6 He asks the Old Testament Church, Where is my honor—where is my fear if I am your Father and Master? He asks the same of us. God's commands are to be honored. Nothing dishonors Him more than when His people who are His prophets, priests and kings despise His covenants and laws. In verse 7 He made it clear that when Israel despised the table of the Lord they proved they really despised Him.

God concludes the Old Testament by giving Israel a message of hope they do not deserve. "Behold," He says, "I am going to send My messenger [John the Baptist] . . . . and the Lord, whom you seek, will suddenly come to His temple" (Mal. 3:1). Between this time and the coming of Jesus Christ, recorded in the New Testament, the Church of the Old Testament sat in great darkness for over four hundred years, "swallowed up among the heathen nations."

How many of the Church's illnesses and weaknesses are caused by the sin of unequal marriage, we can never imagine. The effects are so far-reaching, for generations to come.

8

SHE DECIDED TO MARRY AN UNBELIEVER

(This account is true with only
the names of the persons changed.)

The phone call which would afterward toll in Mary's mind like a death knell brought tragic news one beautiful spring day, news which foreshadowed one of the most difficult times Mary and Bob would ever face.

Mary cheerfully answered the phone. It was Ginny, their 25-year-old daughter, graduate student at the University.

"Mommy," she lilted, "remember John, the charming doctorate student I told you about?"

"Why, yes, I do," Mary answered.

"Well, Mommie, I'm having dinner with him tonight. I've already mentioned to you how fascinating and brilliant he is, but I do feel scared."

"Perhaps you have good reason to feel scared."

"Why?"

"Well, for one thing, do you know what he believes?"

"I'm . . . not sure,"

"Is He Muslim, Coptic, or a true Christian who loves Jesus as Saviour?"

"I don't know," Ginny answered.

"Do you mean that you, a staunch believer in Christ, are going to date a man whose religious beliefs you do not even know?"

"Mommie, he is so admirable—and so very trustworthy."

Trying to erase from her voice the rising anxiety, Mary said, as evenly as she could, "Can't you see, dear, that you are placing yourself in an extremely vulnerable position, and very likely you'll become involved more deeply with him just because he does have so many admirable and attractive qualities?"

A slight chill edging her lowered voice, Ginny answered slowly, "Who said that I don't want to be involved?"

"What did you say?" Mary faintly asked, her mind reeling.

Ginny didn't answer.

Mary's heart screamed in anguish, "Oh, God, what is she saying? What is our child, our first covenant child, saying to me? Tell me Lord, that it isn't so . . . these words she says to me. Oh, strengthen me so that I can answer her sensibly."

"Ginny . . . you say you love Jesus . . . have always said so from the time you were a little thing. Will you make sure that you consider all that you know to be true about dating or marrying unbelievers? What God asks you? It could be that John does truly believe in Christ as his Saviour. I pray that this is so, but you should be sure of this before you even go out with him. You are scared. And I am more than scared for you. I am terrified, because you seem so serious about this man. Intellectually you and he have so much in common. And you say that he's truthworthy and kind and gentle. Already you are admiring him before you have even considered what he believes, which is the most important thing of all. You are *already* involved."

"Now, Mommie, don't worry so much," Ginny tried to reassure her mother. But Mary, knowing Ginny's serious nature, felt in her heart that the die was already cast. For all her reassurances, Ginny seemed adamant. Mary knew that their conversation was at an end as far as Ginny was concerned. Indeed, there was nothing more for Mary to say either. She hung up with great foreboding.

That night Mary and Bob and the rest of the family prayed earnestly that God would work in the hearts of Ginny and John, working out His perfect will as sovereign Lord.

Weeks went by. Ginny continued to date John. By now John had assured Ginny that he had had an experience of the presence of Someone or Something which was with him once when he was critically ill. He preferred to call this presence "Jesus." He told her that his experience of this contentless Christ was just as valid as hers or her parents'. Gradually Ginny came to believe that it was just as valid but that they just expressed their experience in a different way.

So, since Mary and Bob hadn't been able to talk with John personally about his faith, they were overjoyed when sometime later Ginny told her mother that John did truly believe in Christ as his Saviour. Ginny knew her Reformed doctrine well; they had confidence in her judgment, and even though there was still some uneasiness of heart they could not explain, they accepted with praise her evaluation of John's faith.

Ginny brought John home on only one or two very brief visits involving pleasantries and small talk. Mary and Bob had no opportunity to talk with John about spiritual things. And the inexplicable, intuitive uneasiness of heart continued.

Soon, in the middle of a busy morning, the telephone jangled its insistent summons. Mary quickly set aside the bread dough she was kneading, hurriedly washed and dried her hands and sped across the kitchen to answer.

“Hi, Mom, it’s Ginny. Are you and Dad going to be at home tonight? If you are,” Ginny’s excited voice rushed on, “John and I will be over for a while. John’s much impressed with your and Dad’s faith in Christ and would like to talk with you. And, Mom, there is something else we want to talk about with both of you—a surprise!” “How is everybody?” she asked breathlessly.

Before Mary could answer, Ginny was saying, “Bye. See you all tonight then?”

“Yes, dear, see you tonight.”

Ginny’s voice was enthusiastic and confident; Mary’s was weak and faltering as she struggled with the rush of disquieting thoughts stirred by Ginny’s call. Maybe John really is a believer who truly loves Jesus as Saviour and Lord, she hopefully told herself. Maybe he is truly interested in the Reformed interpretation of those beliefs. Oh, I hope so. Lord, quiet my thoughts and please give Dad and me the grace and wisdom to meet any crisis. For Mary knew almost instinctively the “something else,” the *surprise*, Ginny and John wished to talk about was their desire to marry.

Still sitting by the phone, dimly aware of her wildly thudding heart, the bread dough forgotten, Mary let pictures of Ginny’s childhood parade through her troubled mind: Ginny being baptized, Mary and Bob proud and serious as they assumed their covenant obligations for their new baby; Ginny at three, lisping Bible verses and answering the catechism question “Who made you?” with “God made me and all ‘sings’ ”; Ginny talking of Jesus’ love to her little friends; eleven-year-old Ginny with her sure sense of fair play and justice which sometimes incurred the anger of her peers; teenage Ginny discussing spiritual things at family devotion, making public profession of her faith in Christ, teaching Bible Club for eight-year-olds; college-age Ginny introducing her classmates to Christ, yet sometimes struggling with her own doubts when confronted with false philosophies; graduate-school Ginny opening her apartment for students to be taught Van Til’s doctrines of the Reformed faith. (It was at this time Ginny met John on campus.)

With great effort Mary put down her fears, fixed herself a cup of tea and made dessert for the evening, reasoning that genuine hospitality, as much as anything else, contributes to ease of conversation and communication.

That evening Mary and Bob and Ginny and John sat around the kitchen table. Ginny smiling broadly, said, “I imagine you’ve already guessed what our surprise is. You tell them, John.”

John smiled at Bob. "Ginny and I are ready to marry and would like your permission and blessing."

Bob graciously told him he would be glad to give his blessing, and, as a father who took his covenant obligation seriously, he would be glad to give his covenant daughter to a man who had been born again and believed that Jesus Christ was his only substitute for sin, dying for him in his place on the cross. Mary told John that Ginny had told her than he did believe in Christ as his Saviour and that they were glad.

John then explained to Mary and Bob what he meant by believing in Christ: how he thought he had experienced the presence of Christ when he was seriously ill; how this constituted his *new birth* in that he looked upon life differently now. He said that he did not believe in original sin, nor in the historical fact that Christ had died on a cross outside Jerusalem, nor, of course, in the historical, physical resurrection of Christ. His experience, as Mary and Bob brokenheartedly saw, was not based on the infallible Word of God but only on his feelings. Mary and Bob sat there appalled—appalled and angry at their covenant child for drawing this fine young man into a situation of confusion and bewilderment. And *hurt*. John indeed was hurt so much that Mary and Bob feared that he must have felt totally rejected by their shock and silence.

They then talked with him at length, explaining that their faith in Christ was based upon absolutes of God's Word. Ginny angrily accused them of wanting John to speak of his faith only in the Reformed terms by which they expressed their faith. She was hurt and grieved and furious, but she gave no indication that her confidence in the validity of John's faith was shaken, that John's faith was at all different from hers or her parents' faith. He was just stating his faith differently, that was all, she said.

At this point Bob felt that the best way to calm all of the mixed emotions and reactions was to pray. He could not give his blessing to their marriage, but he could ask his sovereign God to bring order and glory to Himself out of the jumbled confusion.

Bob urged Ginny and John to have a talk with the pastor and elders of Ginny's church. Bob knew that he and Mary, as well as Ginny and John, needed the pastor's and session's coolheaded, objective appraisal. John agreed to this, but, after a long talk with the pastor, decided that "the church had nothing to offer him," the Reformed faith, in particular. Two elders talked with Ginny. One, with his arm about her shoulders, lovingly besought her not to marry John. But she was resolute, though at one point in a moment of uncertainty, she did write John a letter saying that they had better reconsider.

But John only pursued her more ardently than ever, finally convincing her for good that he was a child of God in the same way she was.

So they set the marriage date. John chose the church to be married in, but not Ginny's church.

Bob had told Ginny that if she planned to go through with her marriage to an unbeliever, he would not be able to give her away, nor could he in Christian conscience attend her wedding. He said that as an elder in the Church of Christ he could not come, and as a covenant father he could not encourage her to marry an unbeliever—not even by his presence at her wedding. As an elder he believed that he had obligations to God and to the body of Christ as well as a responsibility to set a good example to other parents and in particular to other covenant children who might be tempted to follow her example if Bob and Mary encouraged their daughter in any way to disobey God's law. They both felt that their presence at the ceremony would imply unspoken or partial agreement with their covenant child's decision.

John was incredulous, accusing them of virtually torturing their daughter. Mary, with tenderest sympathy for his anguish, explained, "What you do not understand, John, is that Dad and I love Jesus more than we do our beloved child. We must obey Him and do His will before we do her will. We cannot really expect you to understand. And we are sorry for your pain. But we are not binding your conscience by trying to force you to do something you know is wrong, and we ask only that you do not bind our conscience by your accusations."

Bob told John that he respected his honesty in that he did not make a false profession of faith couched in words acceptable to their position or to the session. Bob and Mary knew with certainty now where he stood, but Ginny was still convinced that his profession of faith was an acceptable one to God. She was crushed by her parents decision not to participate in her marriage. "I never thought, Mom, I would live to see the day you would do such a thing to me," she said with great grief upon her face.

"And Dad and I never thought for a moment you would do such a thing to your Lord and to us, Ginny. God is more grieved than any of us."

Bob and Mary sorrowed and yet they hoped, hoped that something would change the situation which they knew could not have God's blessing. They thought of their daughter's spiritual welfare and knew in their hearts that her marriage would take her farther away from the Lord unless God performed a work of grace in John's heart soon. They prayed that that might be so. Mary said that she had not suffered so deeply since her beloved father's death. A pall seemed to hang over the whole family. As Mary said, "It seems to Bob and me that Ginny is committing spiritual suicide. That is worse than physical death."

Bob and Mary reflected upon all of the efforts which had been made to deflect Ginny from proceeding with marriage to John. Was there anything else they could do? they asked themselves. Maybe a letter of thoughtful persuasion and reassurance of their love? Indeed, they had come to love John very dearly in these past few months, so maybe a letter could, at this last moment, be the answer. Ginny might be able to be a little more objective if she could quietly read a letter alone without the distraction of her parents' presence. Mary and Bob decided what they would say, what approach they would make and the reassurance they would give. They sent the following letter to Ginny and a copy to John so that he would know their concern for him and would not feel left out:

Dearest Ginny,

Thoughts of you and John have occupied our minds almost constantly. Our prayers for both of you are almost never-ending. But it isn't our thoughts and prayers we write to reassure you of, important as they are. It is necessary to reassure you of our love which at present you seem to feel we lack.

It is difficult indeed to explain love in words, as John says, because our words may be misunderstood and misinterpreted. But, are not acts misunderstood, misinterpreted, misjudged?

It is most difficult indeed to explain love in words because our decision not to attend your wedding has cast doubt in your mind as to our love for you. It seems we have failed when talking with you to make it clear what great love is involved in our decision. This is why we believe a letter might more effectively tell you our love for you.

It's hard to know where to begin. Let's begin at your baptism. It was here that we assumed our obligations, under our God in Christ, to you as our covenant child. You were our child in Christ—a holy seed not because of human parentage, but holy seed because both of your parents were united to Christ by His shed blood, the blood of the everlasting Covenant. We vowed to train you as a covenant child, instructing you in the Word of God, praying with and for you, talking of Christ as we worked and played and ate and lay down at night. Then we rejoiced as parents when, in childlike simplicity, you spoke the name of Jesus in real love and sang a child's praises to God. We were even happier when you publicly acknowledged Christ as Lord and Saviour and united with the church. From that time until the present, or, rather, until the moment you become John's, we are still accountable to God as covenant parents, and you are accountable to God as a covenant child, even though you are twenty-five.

At this point you seem convinced that Christ is pleased with your decision to marry, and you intensely desire that we have the same conviction. We believe that John earnestly desires the same thing. At first, we took your word that John held to the same faith that we hold and that you hold. We were sublimely happy because we knew well what your faith in Christ had always been. We knew that *you* knew what is involved doctrinally and experientially. So we believed you when you said you were convinced John is born again. At this juncture, had you married John without our knowing it, we would have believed that you had married one who has the same saving faith in Christ which you have.

But now we have talked at length with John. We now *know* what he believes. Both of you earnestly contend that no two faiths are ever the same. Though we admit that each individual *experiences* faith, and even *expresses* faith, in different ways, we cannot admit, on the basis of Scripture, that there is more than one faith—*the* faith. We agree with Jude, earnestly contending for *the* faith which was *once* delivered to the saints. The content, the presuppositions of this faith never change because the Word of God never changes. We cannot deny this faith which basically is faith in the substitutionary death of Christ for our sins. This confession of Christ as Redeemer and Saviour and the Substitute for sin, reconciling us to God, is the only confession of faith pleasing to the Father, Son, and Holy Spirit.

When one cannot make this confession, he is actually rejecting the Son as Saviour and Lord, despising the Father's unspeakable gift to us, and grieving the Holy Spirit beyond comprehension. This causes Dad and me inexplicable grief. What human sorrow is greater than the sorrow a Christian feels for the soul of another who rejects the saving grace of Christ? It is greater sorrow than any sorrow we can feel for the most awful physical or mental suffering of man, or for death itself—and greater love, too, is involved in such concern.

The love Dad and I feel (as well as the love of the Session and Pastor) for the souls of you and John is a love given to us by Christ. It is this love that impels us to make this present decision. As covenant parents we must not betray our responsibility to Christ and His Bride, the Church. We must not deceive you or John by seeming to give assent to the union of our believing covenant child to one who, at this time, cannot say that he is "justified by the blood of Christ, and shall be saved from wrath through him"; that "when he was yet a sinner Christ died for him"; that "when he was an enemy, he was reconciled to God by the death of his Son"; that "Jesus came to save sinners"; that he is "not redeemed with corruptible things as silver and gold, from his vain conversation received by tradition from your fathers; but with the precious blood of Christ, as of a lamb without blemish and without spot; who was foreordained before the foundation of the world, but was manifest in these last times for you,who by Him do believe in God."

You see, dear, John would not admit to any of the above truths of Scripture. It is on that basis that we judge him to be an unbeliever.

Dad and I love you dearly. You know that. But in the confusion and hurt you doubt our love. We love you fervently. Peter says that when our souls are purified in obeying the truth through the Spirit unto unfeigned love of the brethren, we are to see that we love one another with a pure heart fervently; being born again not of corruptible seed, but of incorruptible, by the Word of God, which lives and abides forever.

This love given to Dad and me for you came by grace alone through faith in the shed blood of Christ. It is this gift of unfeigned love we give to you and John. We do love both of you with the love of Christ. There is no greater love. It is this love,for Christ and for you, which prevents us at the present time from directly or indirectly giving our unqualified blessing to your marriage. You have involved our love in Christ for you by your love for each other. Each of us is honestly trying to follow his own conscience. We have tried to tell each other why we can or cannot do certain things. And in the process we have caused great questioning of mind, and pain to each other's consciences, but the fact remains that we must make only those decisions which square with the Word of God so that our consciences will not be violated and we are thereby found guilty of sinning against our Christian conscience. Each of us is responsible to God.

Our love for you in Christ demands that we give you only to one who is reconciled to God through the blood of Christ. Through His blood we are one with Him, united in the bonds of His love. "Without the shedding of blood is no remission of sin." "How much more shall the blood of Christ, who through the eternal Spirit offered himself without spot to God, purge your conscience from dead works to serve the living God?" (Hebrews 9:14, 22).

We earnestly and humbly beseech God that John may come to know Christ in saving faith. John says that maybe in the future he can say that which would please us. (Our concern is not so much that he please us as that he please God.) We remind him that "*now* is the day of salvation." There may not be a tomorrow. The Scriptures say, "It is a fearful thing to fall into the hands of the living God." "For if we sin wilfully after that we have received the knowledge of the truth, there remaineth no more sacrifice for sins." "He that despised Moses' law died without mercy under two or three witnesses; of how much sorer punishment, suppose ye shall he be thought worthy, who hath trodden under foot the Son of God, and hath counted the blood of the covenant wherewith he was sanctified, an unholy thing, and hath done despite unto the Spirit of Grace?"

That is a fearful question, Ginny. Oh, how we hope that John seriously considers these claims of Christ. If he does not consider them now, you have no right to assume that he ever will. We cannot presume upon God's grace.

You know these truths so well. John is not yet born into the family of God. You are, you say. Just as you are our own flesh and blood, so you are Christ's flesh and blood because you are born again, born into the family of God. John is not yet one of God's family. Dad and I can give you only to a child of God.

We hope we have conveyed the depth of our love for you in Christ. Words are inadequate to tell you. We only point to Christ whose love we not only strive to pattern and follow, but whose love we have and know by faith in His Word.

John had said that we cannot be sure just what words mean—even the Word of God. He seems to believe that Scripture, as well as what anyone says, may be a matter of private interpretation—a matter of semantics. We hope that you will not by any mechanics of semantics read into or interpret what we have written to you to mean that we do not love you with all our heart; we pray that you will not feel that our position is an act that speaks louder than all of the words of love we have written and spoken to you now and in the past. We hope that you can see our love in Christ as we know it—a love for you both which we try in His name and for His sake to keep free of dissimulation, hypocrisy or deceit; a love which yearns for your souls. Outward appearance, concern for things, and other conditions of life—even marriage—while important, are not of comparable importance as your souls.

You have made your decision. John is the man you are going to marry. Now we know for whom we have prayed long before he ever became a reality in your life and ours—even while he was a little boy. We prayed that God would prepare a husband for you. In His inscrutable wisdom and mysterious way He has sent John your way and you have wrongly decided to make him your life's partner. God, for some reason unknown to us is permitting you to do this, but you must know that your marriage will not have His approval because it violates His command to marry only a believer.

We believe this as covenant parents and we will bow to God's permissive will. As loving parents we must also bow before Him in obedience never to encourage our children in willful disobedience to His direct commands. We can only act insofar as God commands us. At present we have gone as far as we can conscientiously go.

But we will always pray for you and we will always love both of you now, and—we hope—in eternity.

With tenderest love,
Mother and Dad

Well, John and Ginny went on with their plans, without Mary and Bob. Occasionally Ginny stopped by after shopping. She showed her sisters and Mary her new pink wedding slippers. "Aren't they a lovely color?" she asked. Mary, choking on tears, nodded and later wept. Ginny showed her the beautiful rose-printed silk for her wedding gown. "Isn't it gorgeous?" "Yes," Mary answered, "It is beautiful." Later she wept again. It seemed that was all she did for weeks, in spite of the fact that she and Bob knew God was in control of the whole situation—*that* they never doubted, for they both had confidence in their sovereign God. Yet, to both Mary and Bob, from a human viewpoint, it did seem strange that God would work in just this way to show His glory.

The wedding day arrived. Mary and Bob did not get to see Ginny at all that day. Relatives came to the house after the wedding. May of them were Christians who saw nothing wrong in attending the marriage of a believer to an unbeliever. In fact, Mary and Bob got little support from many of them; instead, they were criticized for taking such a firm stand—criticized harshly by unbelievers and reproached by some Christians. It was implied that they were heartless and unloving in refusing to cooperate in the most important day of their daughter's life. Just after the wedding, Bob's mother reproved Mary, saying firmly, "You should have gone to the wedding, Mary." Mary fled the room, weeping again.

But the pastor and the elders thanked Mary and Bob for putting God first. The pastor told them that they would never know how much it meant to him, to the Church and to the session that they had decided not to encourage their child in wrongdoing. And though many criticized, there were fellow church members who expressed their gratitude for such an example of Christian courage.

And it did take courage—more courage and faith than Bob or Mary ever felt they could muster. Mary said that it was the most painful, difficult decision of their lives, but a decision which gave peace with God in obedience to Him. Their decision brought suffering, and great fear that their beloved child and her husband would be alienated from them. But God did not allow that to happen—not entirely. Their relationship with both children is really very fine now—in most respects. Mary says "in most respects" because, as we know, a relationship of belief with unbelief can never be completely full or perfect. There is always some alienation present, but that is not because of Bob's and Mary's decision. It is the result of sin which always alienates people from each other.

What of the marriage nearly fourteen years after? Has it lasted? Yes, to all appearances. Is it Christian? No, to all appearances. They do not talk about God or Jesus or spiritual things, at least not to Bob and Mary nor to the rest of the family. They do not, as far as is known, pray with and for their children. They are members of a liberal denomination. John is an elder. Ginny sings in the choir and participates in other church activities, one of which is counseling. The children attend Sunday School, though how faithfully, Mary and Bob do not know.

Ginny's Christian sister-in-law sent the children a Bible story book. John resents his children reading that Adam and Eve were historical figures who fell in the Garden of Eden. He thinks that the doctrine of original sin is heinous. Both of the children seem to show some interest in spiritual things. Mary and Bob and the family pray that God will give His grace to them.

They trust God's promise that He will bring glory to His name through this marriage, in His own inscrutable way. They know that God will work out His own will according to His good pleasure, and that all will be well. God is perfect and so is His will.

9

WHAT MUST WE THEN DO?

"He will remember His covenant forever" (Ps. 111:5b).

Forever . . . . Forever God remembers His covenant with us that we belong to Him alone. He has ordained it forever. "Holy and awesome is His name. The fear of the Lord is the beginning of wisdom."

Psalm 112:1, 2 starts with a doxology to the Lord. Then follows the assurance to us that if we fear the Lord our children and grandchildren will be blessed.

Parents and children, pastors and sessions are bound to covenant responsibilities. We parents whose covenant children are deciding to marry must remember our part of the covenant. We still have a responsibility to our children to pray for them and to guide them in honoring and glorifyng the Lord, just as we promised to do when we had them baptized into the name of our triune God, the Father, the Son, and the Holy Ghost. They are *His* children. We cannot expect the verses above to apply to our descendants nor can we expect God to make our grandchildren mighty *in the Lord* if we in any way encourage our children to marry *out of the Lord.*

God plainly says that the sins of grandparents and of their children are visited upon the third and fourth generations. An unbelieving mate causes his or her children to sin against the Lord. It is inevitable that this is so . The children see the division between the beliefs of father and mother and they go limping between two opinions. Sometimes, in their confusion they give up their faith—maybe temporarily, or, more tragically, what appears to be permanently.

Surely grandparents of the children of such a union should have thought twice before they let misplaced sympathy and emotions influence them into acceptance of an unequally yoked marriage. And we do get emotional! From the day we hear our son or daughter tell us of an impending marriage to an unbeliever, we begin to rationalize, and to make plans, especially when it becomes evident that no argument or pleading will dissuade them from marriage. Our minds reel as our thoughts conjure up the unsettling pictures of the future because of our child's decision: *Perhaps I should cooperate more. . . . We must not alienate our child . . . . What will people think if we don't go to the wedding? . . . The children may never speak to us again . . . . We may never be allowed to see our grandchildren . . . . Maybe God will save the unbelieving one anyway . . . especially if we show*

Christian understanding and are sweet and loving. And all the while we feel guilty.

This is the way *we* think. In our grief and emotional reaction, we compromise our beliefs and go against our conscience when we know that God has different thoughts on the matter. God has forbidden us to give our daughters or sons to "heathen."

Maybe that seems like a severe word to use, but really that is what an unbeliever is, God says: a heathen, an enemy of God. His God is *not* our God—the God of our Lord and Saviour Jesus Christ. He is not committed to our God at all. Jeremiah 9:26 calls all uncircumcised nations "heathen." They did not have the sign and seal of union with God: circumcision.

Now there is no Christian parent who will grant his child every desire, but now and then in moments of lenience or even fear we give in to some sinful decisions. Perhaps in no other activity of our children do we go farther in compromising our stand than in this area of marriage to one far from our Christ. Somehow we don't seem to regard this act of disobedience as serious as, say, robbery or arson, or murder.

Let's consider a "suppose" case. Suppose your child came to you and said, "Mom. Dad. I need more money for school. There is no possible way I can earn enough myself and you don't have it to give to me. I'm desperate, so I've decided to take some money from a bank. They have plenty to spare. But I will need you to help me. Dad, you will cover for me. Mom, you'll drive the get-away car. Don't let me down . . . please. This is my last chance. I know you love me and will do anything for me."

It is a foregone conclusion you wouldn't cooperate. Right? Ridiculous even to ask, you answer. Yet when it comes to mismatched marriages of believer to unbeliever, so many Christian parents in Bible-believing churches say, "Yes, we'll stand by you, our child. We would never let you down." And even though they know the marriage is wrong, they are often angry with a faithful pastor (or session or loving friends) who, out of love for Christ, refuses to marry their boy or girl to one who does not love Christ.

I do not mean to be harsh with believing parents. Perhaps there is hardly any decision our children make that so tugs at our heartstrings. The visions of our little girl as a bride adorned in her white gown and veil, the beautiful ceremony of marriage, our conviction that this is the most important day in her life, and that we *must* give her our support, often overwhelm our former resolves to do what is right no matter the cost. We decide that the cost is too high to pay even though we are literally torn apart as we see our children settle for a lifetime with one at odds with their God and ours. We see so much division looming up in the future: a drifting from their faith; a drifting from us, from the Church, from Christian influence. Our fearful thoughts run amok: *How can we mend what is done? How can we heal alienation bound to occur?*

Well, we can't mend and heal by disobeying God. It never works. No matter how deeply Christ sympathizes with us and our child, He will only honor Christian parents with His approval when we do what is right. Our emotions and our sentiments must not be our criteria for settling such a vital question. It must never be settled on how *we feel* or how our *children feel* but on what *God says* about this union. What *does* He say? What are *His* commands? Remember He makes commands of us and our children in this matter—commands in the Old Testament and commands in the New Testament.

I believe a case might be made that Samson's parents were guided by their emotions, fear, perhaps, when they cooperated in Samson's marriage to a Philistine woman![1]

Samson, who was not only an Israelite but a Nazarite, made his first bad choice when he went down to Timnath and saw a daughter of the Philistines. He went home and peremptorily ordered his father and mother, "I saw a woman in Timnah, one of the daughters of the Philistines; now, therefore, get her for me as a wife." Perhaps our first thought is that he could be commended for telling his parents at all, but upon second thought, in those days he could hardly sneak away secretly to procure a wife without his parents' cooperation and consent. A bridegroom needed a dowry (either the groom or his father paid it) to give to the bride's father to induce him to give her in marriage.

Samson's father and mother asked him, "Is there no woman among the daughters of your relatives, or among all our people that you go to take a wife from the uncircumcised Philistines?" They were worried that their child who had been set aside by God for His purposes would consider marrying a heathen who did not love God. But at this point Samson no longer cared if he pleased God, so, of course, he no longer cared if he pleased his parents.

"Get her for me," he ordered his parents, "for she looks good to me."

Now it is true that Samson's sinful choice was going to be used of the Lord to occasion aggression on the Philistines. This shows how God

[1]Could it be they feared him because he was so huge and strong?

overrules our sin and can bring good of it. But that in no wise relieved Samson of his responsibility to do what God commanded. And though his parents may have known that God *could* bring good from evil, they did not know that he *would.* If they had known for certain that God would bring the defeat of their enemies through Samson's marriage to one of them, no doubt they would have excused their cooperation in their son's plans. Their complicity in their son's sinful marriage could not be defended by saying it was God's will. Apparently without further thought they went down to Timnath just as Samson told them to. Samson got his way. His parents cooperated.

How many of God's people must have asked their child the same question Samson's parents asked him: Is there no woman among the daughters of God's Church that you take an unbelieving wife from a family who cares nothing for the Lord, nothing for His interests? *Why* have you made such a decision? is the usual question.

I think we ask the wrong question when we ask, Why? I believe with Jay Adams that we should not ask *why*, but we should ask *what.*[2] *What* is this thing you are doing? That question always makes us face the fact of our sin because it leaves us no room for theorizing or rationalizing our decisions. The question, "*What* are you doing?" forces us to confess our action. We face our sin, and then the question of *why* we did it can more easily be answered.

In spite of his parents' concern, Samson, like many a believing child, pursued his plan to see the unbeliever and then to marry her. His father, for the second time, went down to Timnath with him going along with his plans. At the wedding feast Samson propounded a riddle to 30 Philistine companions, promising them gifts of clothing if they could answer the riddle. They asked Samson's wife to get the answer from Samson, threatening her and her father with burning if she wouldn't comply.

Samson's Philistine wife, not raised in the truth and pressured by fear, betrayed him. She used wily tactics to learn the riddle of the lion and honey, weeping and whining, "You only hate me, and you do not love me; you have propounded a riddle to the sons of my people, and have not told it to me."

He said to her, "Behold, I have not told it to my father or mother; so should I tell you?" But she continued to weep the whole seven days of their wedding feast—not exactly a fantastic honeymoon!

---

[2]See chapter 26, "Asking Questions," in Jay Adams, *The Christian Counselor's Manual*, (Nutley, NJ: Presbyterian and Reformed Publishing Co., 1973).

Then disaster struck. Samson killed 30 people of Ashkelon. To pay off his bet he gave their clothes to the men who answered his riddle. He then left for his father's house in an ugly, vengeful frame of mind. While there, his wife, who was in Timnath, was given to the one who had been his best man—his friend.

When he visited his wife at harvest time, he took a goat to give her. But his father-in-law would not let him enter her room. Samson, angered even more, justified in his heart the burning of the Philistine grain fields. The Philistines retaliated by burning his father-in-law and Samson's wife. Mad with revenge, Samson ruthlessly slaughtered a great number of Philistines.

So a vicious cycle of rebellion and violence was set up. God did bring good out of it all, but Samson had sinned against God's command nevertheless. He, his wife, and her people reaped a whirlwind.

Samson's next relationship was with a harlot with whom he spent his nights, Delilah who also betrayed him to the Philistines. He lost his great strength and his eyesight (the Philistines put out both his eyes and made him their slave). We don't read that Samson ever made a good marriage.

Just as Samson and his parents were engaged in the struggle between good and evil, so are we today. We parents and our children are caught in a warfare older than man, a warfare between God and Satan; between powers and principalities; between the bride of Christ and the Antichrist. What shall we do?

J. I. Packer, in his beautiful book, *Knowing God,* page 23, says, " . . .*action* taken by those who know God is their *reaction* to the anti-God trends which they see operating around them. While their God is being defied or disregarded, they cannot rest; they feel they must do something; the dishonor done to God's name goads them into *action*" (italics mine).

Every anti-God influence intruding into our Christian life calls for action. If we don't respond as good warriors should, there will be casualties galore: divided homes; painful, bitter relationships; ruined children for coming generations; a weakened Church. The bride will be sickly; the Groom dishonored, the Holy Spirit grieved.

Parents must act. Sessions and pastors must act. Children must act. We must not only act, but we must weep, as Francis Schaeffer says he weeps[3] when he sees a Christian marry an unbeliever.

Parents, how should we react and act when our believing child insists

[3]Dr. Francis Schaeffer, *Genesis in Space and Time* (Downers Grove, Illinois: Inter-Varsity Press, 1972), p. 86.

upon marrying an unbeliever? If you were called to face this trial, would you go immediately to your pastor or elders for counsel, or would you leave them in the dark as to whether your child is seriously dating an unbeliever? Or resolved to marry one? Do you consider it no one else's concern? Or think you do not need spiritual help to handle the situation? Or feel that it is a personal, private family matter?

Well, if you do feel that way, I would kindly and sympathetically—though urgently—remind you that the Christian's relationship to Jesus Christ and to every true believer in the bride of Christ transcends your personal, private relationship to your family. God's family has priority over our earthly family. You must take action outside your family in the family of God to which you and your child belong.

What your children do vitally concerns the Church. What they do is of utmost importance to the pastor, the session and the other members. When you and your children joined the church, all of them made a solemn vow to guide, to teach, to pray for you and your children. God knows that we parents *cannot* handle these crises alone. We need all the help we can get since there usually comes a point where we cannot effectively deal with such an emotionally supercharged situation.

We parents must notify our church officers when our child seriously dates an unbeliever, or tell them of our child's intentions to marry one. Our pastors and sessions are commanded by God to speak—always in love—to any erring member of the body of Christ. The scriptural purpose? To lovingly restore the member of Christ's body from sin to a right walk with the Lord; and to keep the body of Christ pure and spotless for her Lord.

The attitude shown by parents to discipline (that's what this loving concern of the elders is called) may determine the woe or well-being of their child's future. Negative, hostile response to pastoral and sessional discipline proves to our child that we scorn the advice and correction of those men appointed by God to care for our souls.

When we parents turn away from correction and side with our children's sinful decisions, we only prove that we are ignorant of the fact that the elders of the church come to us in the authority of God. And we reinforce our child's rebellion and sinful behavior.

David recognized the right of *any* Christians to come to us in love to express to us and our children their concern for any of our sinful actions that mar Christ's body. In Psalm 141:5 David said, "Let the righteous smite me in kindness and reprove me; It is oil upon my head; Do not let my head refuse it."

What is our reaction when Christians come to us with even the slightest, but justifiable, reproof? We usually don't see the kindness. Our proud heads feel only the smiting and we refuse to accept reproof, let alone consider it blessed oil upon our heads—even if the reproof is done in greatest kindness. We are like stubborn Israel more than we care to admit.

An especially serious weakness in our Christian walk, I believe, is in the failure of interaction between church members, pastor and session. Communication is often virtually nil. We members don't make our needs known. We limp along without help. We hate reproof, but a wise man doesn't. Reprove *him* and he will love you, God says.

Certainly not many of us parents and children prove wise when faced with loving discipline. In our 30 some years in Reformed churches, how *many* parents and children we have known who have become angry at loving discipline exercised by the elders over them. It is our private matter, they said. "What are *you* doing invading our privacy?" they asked, in effect. Concern is mistaken for meddling; reproof, for interference in family affairs; firmness, for lack of compassion and understanding. Communication breaks down. Hostility deepens. Often, in anger and rebellion, whole families cut their ties with the local church or the entire denomination. Irreparable damage is done to lives and the body of Christ.

Ezra and Nehemiah, contemporaries living in the final days of the Old Testament, saw firsthand the tragedy of wedding belief and unbelief. They knew that the only unifying principle in the Church was obedience to God's truth. In warning and reproving Israel, the Old Testament Church, they were not being intolerant and pigheaded. Nor are pastors, sessions, or other Christians who are upset and grief-stricken when a fellow-believer marries out of the Lord.

In Ezra's time things were going much better for the people of God. The temple was rebuilt. Their enemies had even become friendly. We hear of no oppression, persecution or war. But something terrible was going on nevertheless. Satan, who never loses an opportunity to destroy the Church was using the friendliness of enemies to hurt the Church. The people of Israel mingled with those who didn't love God and "did according to their abominations"; they took enemy daughters to be their wives and their sons' wives.

God had called them His peculiar, set apart people. Yet once more they showed their contempt for their covenant standing with God. They exposed themselves to idolatry and their covenant children to spiritually divided homes. They were repeating the same sins which had before been the ruin of their Church and nation—not just a few Israelites, but, saddest to say, many priests and Levites were guilty, too. And the princes and rulers had been the chief offenders in this sin which God calls an "abomination." That is, God Himself was filled with loathing.

Princes should be foremost in leading people to do what is right. They have power to prevent wrongdoing. And so do we as kings and queens under our sovereign God, as members of His kingdom. We must lead in setting a good example, especially in marriage. We must never be the stumbling block in the path of one of God's children.

Ezra sorrowed for the sin done against God and for the people who had sinned. He was appalled, so appalled that he had to sit down. He must have been nearly in a state of shock. He feared God's just wrath against Israel. He sorrowed as a mother for the loss of her first-born child. Why? Because he knew the Church was in grave danger. Ezra's grief so affected the members of Israel that many trembled at the words of the God of Israel because of this sin.

Then Ezra fell on his knees and stretched out his hands to God and made one of the most beautiful and moving prayers I have ever read (Ezra 9:6–15):

> O, my God, I am ashamed and embarrassed to lift up my face to Thee, my God, for our iniquities have risen above our heads, and our guilt has grown even to the heavens. Since the days of our fathers to this day we have been in great guilt, and on account of our iniquities we, our kings and our priests have been given into the hand of the kings of the lands, to the sword, to captivity, and to plunder and to open shame, as it is this day. But now for a brief moment grace has been shown from the Lord our God, to leave us an escaped remnant and to give us a peg in His holy place, that our God may enlighten our eyes and grant us a little reviving in our bondage. For we are slaves; yet in our bondage, our God has not forsaken us, but has extended lovingkindness to us in the sight of the kings of Persia, to give us reviving to raise up the house of our God, to restore its ruins, and to give us a wall in Judah and Jerusalem. And now, our God, what shall we say after this? For we have forsaken Thy commandments, which Thou hast commanded by Thy servants the prophets, saying, "The land which you are entering to take possession of it is an unclean land with the uncleanness of the peoples of the lands, with their abominations which have filled it from end to end and with their impurity. So now do not give your daughters to their sons nor take their daughters to

your sons, and never seek their peace or their prosperity, that you may be strong and eat the good things of the land and leave it as an inheritance to your sons forever." And after all that has come upon us for our evil deeds and our great guilt, since Thou our God hast requited us less than our iniquities deserve, and hast given us an escaped remnant as this, shall we again break Thy commandments and intermarry with the peoples who commit these abominations? Wouldst Thou not be angry with us to the point of destruction, until there is no remnant nor any who escape? Our Lord God of Israel,Thou are righteous, for we have been left an escaped remnant, as it is this day; behold, we are before Thee in our guilt, for no one can stand before Thee because of this.

What happened after Ezra prayed and wept and prostrated himself before the house of God? Why, a great congregation of men, women and even children assembled and wept bitterly, too. If we, by God's grace, see the horror of this sin as plainly as Ezra and Nehemiah did, we will weep for this sin among ourselves. Did you weep and pray like Ezra when some Christian boy or girl violated God's command to marry only in the Lord? Or did you rationalize, making excuses for that young person, telling yourself: *Well, these things happen*? Ezra wept. So should we when we see our dear Christian young people make such a tragic mistake. I truly believe that if we spiritually perceive the tragedy, we will weep, and we will welcome instead of condemn our elders and Christian friends when they reprove in order to restore us.

How are we to restore each other? Gently. Lovingly. Humbly. Compassionately. Tenderly. Galatians 6:1–2 tells us: "Brethren, even if a man is caught in any trespass, you who are spiritual [Christian brothers and sisters], restore such a one in a spirit of gentleness; looking to yourself, lest you too [or your own children] be tempted. Bear one another's burdens, and thus fulfill the law of Christ."

When told of marriages of believers to unbelievers, Ezra and Nehemiah both reacted to the sin of the people. Ezra, in horror and grief, pulled out his own hair and tore his robe and mantle—symbolic acts to show his pain for their sin. Nehemiah reacted with violent, righteous indignation when he saw the effects of mixed marriages. He says, "So I contended with them . . . and struck some of them and pulled out their hair, and made them swear by God, 'You shall not give your daughters to their sons, nor take of their daughters for your sons or for yourselves. Did not Solomon king of Israel sin regarding these things? Yet among the many nations there was no king like him, and he was loved by his God, and God made him king over all Israel; nevertheless the foreign women caused even him to sin. Do we then hear about you that you have committed all this great evil by acting unfaithfully against our God by marrying foreign women?' " (Neh. 13:25-27).

Nehemiah said that even the grandson of one of the high priests, Eliashib, had married a daughter of Sanballat the Horonite, one of Israel's deadliest foes. The last prayer he makes is for Eliashib and his grandson and then for himself.

How glad we should be that we live in New Testament times. If we are incensed by the loving, humble reproof of fellow Christians, what would we be like under blows and hair pulling, no matter how much deserved? Paul tells us why discipline must be taken and sin reproved with gentleness and tears. He had written a letter of reproof to God's people. Paul wrote with tears, his big heart broken with love for his people and his Lord.

It is difficult to administer discipline. Tenderhearted elders, pastors and fellow believers always find discipline and godly censure difficult and regrettable.

It is difficult to accept discipline and reproof. But we must. And we must not so insulate ourselves from each other that we can't give or accept discipline. It takes a large measure of the Holy Spirit's grace to give or accept reproof and discipline, but there must be interaction between the giver and the taker to solve mutual problems in the body of Christ. We must be free to guide, reprove and love each other, and we must free each other of the fear of reproving us. We must not shackle those who come to us in Christ's love. We must not hinder by hostility and resentment their God-given ministry to "nouthetically"[4] confront us—to come to us in love and concern in order to help us change.

What shall we then do? Parents? Children?

God tells parents what we must *not* do: "Do not give your daughters to their [unbelievers'] sons; nor shall you take their daughters for your sons." Why? They will turn your sons away from *Me*, God says. He makes it clear that there is only one God to worship and that a covenant with unbelievers leads to other harmful pacts—namely, seducing covenant sons and daughters away from God, causing them to commit spiritual whoredom, which we have discussed before.

[4]See Jay Adam's *Competent to Counsel*, chapter 4, "What Is Nouthetic Counseling?" for explanation of the word *nouthetic*, (Nutley, N.J.: Presbyterian and Reformed Publishing Co., 1970).

Israel sinfully mingled the holy race with the peoples of the land. Princes and rulers were foremost in this. Surely it is a lesson for us who are kings and queens of God's dynasty—Christian parents and children.

We parents must think of our grandchildren as well as of our children. Think of the training they'll get under an unchristian father or mother, training abhorrent to God. Let's not selfishly think only of our love for our own boy or girl, but let's think of Christ and His love for His Church. Ezra tore his robes in anguish over this dreadful situation. He says he was appalled. Are we? Holy seed intermingling with the unholy! How dreadfully this should bear upon our Christian consciences. We cannot violate the laws of nature or the laws of God without fearful consequences.

And children—what shall you then do? Listen to godly parents, your pastor and elders. They have made covenant promises with God to keep in your behalf. And you have covenant obligations, one of which is the mandate to marry none other than a follower of Christ.

If you are a Christian parent groping for guidance, for absolutes, for a point of reference that is constant and true, then look to what God has spoken to you in His Word. We must never do foolish things to please our children or to prove our love for them, or do anything against our Christian conscience just because we are afraid of alienating our children. The world's solutions, based on sentiment, feelings, or custom are not for us unless they are in accord with God's Word. Our world is in serious trouble today, largely because it no longer listens to what God has told us. May God help us Christians not to add to the struggles and confusion of home, Church and society by marrying out of the Lord.

10

EPILOGUE

We all need to love God *more.* We parents must love Him more every day, and then we must help our children to love Him more, to know Him better. J. I. Packer says that the most important thing in the world is to really know God. To know Him better is to love Him more. Knowledge of God—where are we to find it? Obviously, we find it in the revelation He has given of Himself in His Word. If we lack love for Him, it is no doubt because we know so little about Him from His Word. If we lack love for Him, we will make foolish decisions apart from His Word and His will—bad marriages included.

So we must know Him better. That is imperative. I truly think that this lack of knowledge and love on the part of parents and children is the chief reason our children are captivated by worldly, unbelieving mates. God says His people were captured because they had no knowledge (Isa. 5:13). Surely parents and religious leaders were responsible for Israel's ignorance of who their God really was and of who they were themselves. They were princes and princesses, captured because they lacked knowledge of God and of themselves.

You covenant children and we parents are princes and princesses of the dynasty of the Most High God, Creator of the universe. We are to reign with Christ forever. Yet we see many captured by the spirit of the times, lured by deficient love of unbelievers, marrying godless mates who are enemies of their God, of their souls, and of their children.

We parents and our children have been paid the "intolerable compliment" of God, adopted into His family—royalty, we are. It should almost "blow our minds" that we have such nobility conferred upon us. Can you think of yourself as a king or queen in God's kingdom? I can barely rise to such sublime thought myself. But God says it's so; despicable, mean, rebellious creatures, we are given rule and glory with Him, Creator of galaxies without number. Daniel 7:27 says about God's everlasting kingdom: "Then the sovereignty, the dominion, and the greatness of all the kingdoms under the whole heaven will be given to the people of the saints of the Highest One; His kingdom will be an everlasting kingdom, and all the dominions will serve and obey Him."

Don't you think that as members of His kingdom it's high time we Christians who have been given this intolerable compliment of God stop thinking like the present generation of this world? Our age is not a positive age. This age has no absolutes. We are told we must never judge others. But when it comes to wrong, a Christian's mind-set must be different from the world's. We must have a new mind in Christ, a new mind-set conformed to the mold of the Potter. We must (we are commanded to) pass judgment on immorality and sin. We are duty bound to make only right choices.

Truly our sovereign God has been so good to us who share His covenant of grace. In a special love, unparalleled by any known love of man, He has taken us into an everlasting covenant with Himself. He will not break that covenant because He is immutable—changeless! He has honored us as He has honored no other creatures in heaven or earth with the exception of His only begotten Son. In order to keep our feet from slipping, I think we believers just have to remind ourselves over and over again of what God has done for us, of who we are in His plan. We forget, just as Israel did. In His indictment upon them for forgetting, God pled: "My people, what have I done to you, and how have I wearied you? Answer Me." He demanded an answer for He had done nothing but good for them, as He reminds them: "Indeed, I brought you up from the land of Egypt and ransomed you from the house of slavery."

And that's exactly what He's done for us: ransomed us from the power of Satan's kingdom and taken us into His own. How could we forget? If we are not to forget, we must always practice the consciousness of who we are in His plan. If you are young or old, and you want to love Him more, keep reminding yourself of what He's done for you and of what He's doing for you now, and of what He's going to continue to do for you in the future. Look at the stars some cloudless night. Count them if you can. They were placed in twinkling glory by His hand. God not only knows their number but He calls each one by name. (My Christian son-in-law, an astronomer, is amazed by this. That's because he sees through the telescopes the endless array of stars in the heavens.) If you belong to Jesus, you are a gleaming gem, like a star, set into the body of Jesus Christ to emblazon His name throughout the universe. The stars will grow cold, but you will shine eternally for Him. God expects great honor to Himself from you. He expects—yes, demands—obedience in *every* area of your life. He expects—yes, demands—you to choose a mate who will shine just as brightly as you should shine for Him. If your husband, he must lead and guide you and your children in the things of the Lord; if your wife, she must support you in leading and guiding your family. You are to be bound to Him in cords of love to praise and adore Him. You are to be tied—united—to your mate, not by romantic love alone (a wonderful gift to be sure) but by His exhaustless, breathtaking, constant love which enchants, delights, strengthens, exhilarates, unifies and sanctifies your marriage. That is what God wants for your marriage and for your children. And this is what your pastor and session and parents (if they are Christian) want for you, too.

In Isaiah 5 God the Father dictates a poem to the honor of His well-beloved Son whom He has made Lord of the vineyard, the vineyard being Israel or the Church. He said: "Let me sing now for my well-beloved a song of my beloved concerning his vineyard." This is what He sang:

My well-beloved had a vineyard on a fertile hill.
And he dug it all around, removed its stones,
And planted it with the choicest vine.
And he built a tower in the middle of it,
And hewed out a wine vat in it;
Then he expected it to produce good grapes,
But it produced only worthless ones . . . .
Judge between Me and My vineyard.
What more was there to do for My vineyard that
    I have not done in it?
Why, when I expected it to produce good grapes did
    it produce worthless ones?
So now let Me tell you what I am going to do to My
    vineyard:
I will remove its hedge and it will be consumed;
I will break down its wall and it will become trampled
    ground.
And I will lay it waste;
  It will not be pruned or hoed,
But briars and thorns will come up.
I will also charge the clouds to rain no rain on it (vv. 1-5).

God has done everything for us that He could possibly do: chosen us, redeemed us and glorified us, making us His own bride. His expectations are not too high nor too hard; He is righteous and very reasonable considering all that He has done for us. What excuse or reason can be given to God when He looks for good grapes and we give Him sour ones? Or when we "disdainfully sniff at" (God's own accusation leveled at Israel) His command to marry only in the Lord and say as Israel did about His requirements, "My how tiresome it is!" (Mal. 1:13).

God wants to protect you from danger. He loves you. He knows that some of our most devastating trials can be in our own homes. He knows that our most implacable enemy may share our table, our bed, even our thoughts. An enemy that close is too much to reckon with. We are told to love our enemies, but it is unthinkably foolish to marry one.

Of most importance, God knows that an unchristian marriage *cannot* glorify Him. As God's own adopted child you are bound to glorify Him alone. You are married to Him. You are to praise Him to everyone, now and forever. He expects this from you as you fulfill His purpose for your life in His plan to become "conformed to the image of Christ." He expects you to marry princes and princesses of God, not as a matter of pride or superiority, but because God says so, and because only a child of God is a fitting, suitable mate to help you become more like Christ—the goal for which God has called you.

Marry only in the Lord, God commands. Is that really too much to ask of you?